How to
Master Skills for the

Second Edition

TOEFL® iBT

WRITING · Basic

DARAKWON

How to
Master Skills for the
Second Edition

TOEFL® iBT
WRITING · Basic

Publisher Kyudo Chung
Editor Sangik Cho
Authors Arthur H. Milch, Denise McCormack
Proofreader Michael A. Putlack
Designers Minji Kim, Hyeonju Yoon

First Published in August 2007 By Darakwon, Inc.
Second edition first published in March 2025 by Darakwon, Inc.
Darakwon Bldg., 211, Munbal-ro, Paju-si, Gyeonggi-do 10881
Republic of Korea
Tel: 02-736-2031 (Ext. 250)
Fax: 02-732-2037

ISBN 978-89-277-8088-5 14740
978-89-277-8084-7 14740 (set)

www.darakwon.co.kr

Photo Credits
Shutterstock.com

Components Main Book / Answer Key / Free MP3 Downloads
7 6 5 4 3 2 1   25 26 27 28 29

Table of
Contents

INTRODUCTION

1 Information on the TOEFL® iBT

A The Format of the TOEFL® iBT

Section	Number of Questions or Tasks	Timing	Score

Reading	**20 Questions**
	
	• **2 reading passages**
	  – with 10 questions per passage
	  – approximately 700 words long each
		35 Minutes	30 Points

Listening	**28 Questions**
	
	• **2 conversations**
	  – 5 questions per conversation
	  – 3 minutes each
	
	• **3 lectures**
	  – 6 questions per lecture
	  – 3-5 minutes each
		36 Minutes	30 Points

Speaking	**4 Tasks**
	
	• **1 independent speaking task**
	  – 1 personal choice/opinion/experience
	  – preparation: 15 sec. / response: 45 sec.
	
	• **2 integrated speaking tasks: Read-Listen-Speak**
	  – 1 campus situation topic
	    reading: 75-100 words (45 sec.)
	    conversation: 150-180 words (60-80 sec.)
	  – 1 academic course topic
	    reading: 75-100 words (50 sec.)
	    lecture: 150-220 words (60-120 sec.)
	  – preparation: 30 sec. / response: 60 sec.
	
	• **1 integrated speaking task: Listen-Speak**
	  – 1 academic course topic
	    lecture: 230-280 words (90-120 sec.)
	  – preparation: 20 sec. / response: 60 sec.
		17 Minutes	30 Points

Writing	**2 Tasks**
	
	• **1 integrated writing task: Read-Listen-Write**
	  – reading: 230-300 words (3 min.)
	  – lecture: 230-300 words (2 min.)
	  – a summary of 150-225 words (20 min.)
	
	• **1 academic discussion task**
	  – a minimum 100-word essay (10 min.)
		30 Minutes	30 Points

B What Is New about the TOEFL® iBT?

- The TOEFL® iBT is delivered through the Internet in secure test centers around the world at the same time.

- It tests all four language skills and is taken in the order of Reading, Listening, Speaking, and Writing.

- The test is about 2 hours long, and all of the four test sections will be completed in one day.

- Note taking is allowed throughout the entire test, including the Reading section. At the end of the test, all notes are collected and destroyed at the test center.

- In the Listening section, one lecture may be spoken with a British or Australian accent.

- There are integrated tasks requiring test takers to combine more than one language skill in the Speaking and Writing sections.

- In the Speaking section, test takers wear headphones and speak into a microphone when they respond. The responses are recorded and transmitted to ETS's Online Scoring Network.

- In the Writing section, test takers must type their responses. Handwriting is not possible.

- Test scores will be reported online. Test takers can see their scores online 4-8 business days after the test and can also receive a copy of their score report by mail.

2 Information on the Writing Section

The Writing section of the TOEFL® iBT measures test takers' ability to use writing to communicate in an academic environment. This section has two writing tasks. For the first writing task, you will read a passage and listen to a lecture and then answer a question based on what you have read and heard. For the second writing task, you will state and support an opinion in an online classroom discussion.

A Types of Writing Tasks

- **Task 1** Integrated Writing Task

  - You will read a short text of about 230-300 words on an academic topic for 3 minutes. You may take notes on the reading passage.

  - After reading the text, you will listen to a lecture discussing the same topic from a different perspective for about 2 minutes. You may take notes on the lecture.

  - You will have 20 minutes to write a 150-to-225-word summary in response to the question.

- **Task 2** Writing for an Academic Discussion Task

  - You will see a discussion board on a university website that comprises two students responding to a question posted by a professor.

  - You will have 10 minutes to read everything and to write a response to the topic in the online post. It should be at least 100 words.

B Types of Writing Questions

- Integrated Writing Task

  – Summarize the points made in the lecture, being sure to explain how they challenge specific claims/ arguments made in the reading passage.
  cf. This question type accounts for almost all the questions that have been asked on the TOEFL® iBT so far.

  – Summarize the points made in the lecture, being sure to explain how they cast doubt on specific points made in the reading passage.

  – Summarize the points made in the lecture, being sure to specifically explain how they answer the problems raised in the reading passage.

- Writing for an Academic Discussion Task

  – Yes or no questions: These questions require you to agree or disagree with a statement.

  – Preference questions: These questions ask you to state a preference between two similar things.

  – Open-Ended questions: These questions ask for your own thoughts or opinions on a broad topic.

C Important Features of Evaluation

- Quality of Response

  In the first task, the quality of the response is about how well you integrate and relate information from the reading and listening materials. In the second task, it is about the relevance and depth of your argument.

- Language Use

  Language use is about the accuracy and range of your grammar and vocabulary. In order to get good grades on the writing tasks, you should be able to use both basic and more complex language structures and choose the appropriate words.

HOW TO USE THIS BOOK

How to Master Skills for the TOEFL® iBT Writing Basic is designed to be used either as a textbook for a TOEFL® iBT writing preparation course or as a tool for individual learners who are preparing for the TOEFL® test on their own. With a total of sixteen units, this book is organized to prepare you for the test by providing you with a comprehensive understanding of the test and a thorough analysis of every question type. Each unit provides a step-by-step program that helps develop your test-taking abilities. At the back of the book are two actual tests of the Writing section of the TOEFL® iBT.

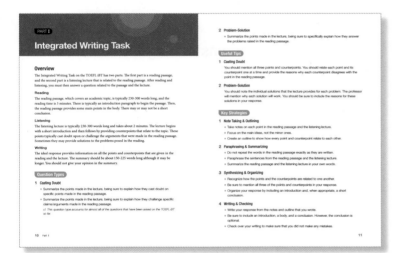

❶ Overview

This section is designed to prepare you for the type of task the part covers. You will be given a full sample question and a model answer in an illustrative structure.

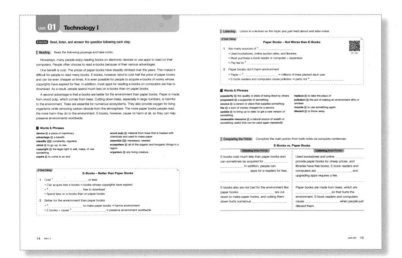

❷ Note Taking & Vocabulary (Integrated Writing Task)

This section provides definitions of difficult words and phrases and also lets you take notes on the passages to make sure that you understand the main points in the passages.

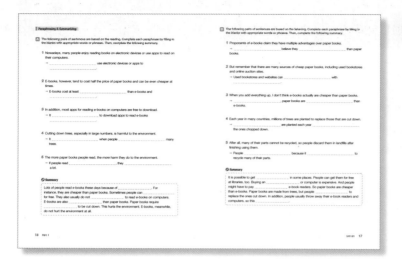

❸ Paraphrasing & Summarizing
(Integrated Writing Task)

This section provides you with the opportunity to paraphrase sentences from the reading and listening passages in order to improve your writing skills. There is also a summary of each passage in which words and phrases must be inserted to complete it.

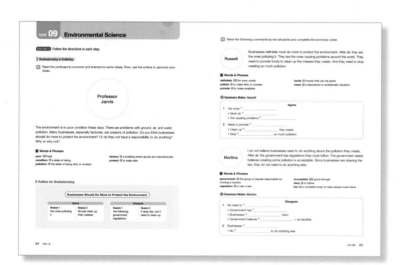

❹ Brainstorming & Outlining
(Writing for an Academic Discussion Task)

This section allows you to brainstorm about the professor's comments and has you complete two outlines to ensure that you understand the responses made by the students.

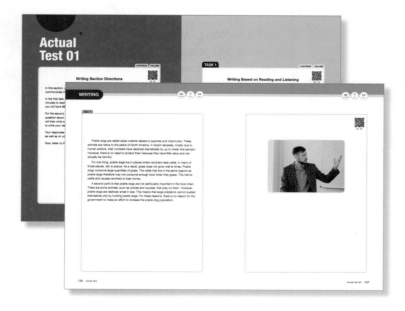

❺ Actual Test

This part will give you a chance to experience an actual TOEFL® iBT test. You will be given two sets of tests that are modeled on the Writing section of the TOEFL® iBT. The topics are similar to those on the real test, as are the questions. This similarity will allow you to develop a sense of your test-taking ability.

PART I

Integrated Writing Task

The integrated writing section consists of one task. You will be presented with a reading passage on a certain topic. Then, you will hear a lecture on the same topic. Typically, the lecture will have a position opposite that of the reading passage. Then, you will be asked a question in which you must write about the arguments made in the listening lecture and the reading passage. You will have 20 minutes to write an essay in response to the question. A typical essay is 150 to 225 words long.

Integrated Writing Task

Overview

The Integrated Writing Task on the TOEFL iBT has two parts. The first part is a reading passage, and the second part is a listening lecture that is related to the reading passage. After reading and listening, you must then answer a question related to the passage and the lecture.

Reading

The reading passage, which covers an academic topic, is typically 230-300 words long, and the reading time is 3 minutes. There is typically an introduction paragraph to begin the passage. Then, the reading passage provides some main points in the body. There may or may not be a short conclusion.

Listening

The listening lecture is typically 230-300 words long and takes about 2 minutes. The lecture begins with a short introduction and then follows by providing counterpoints that relate to the topic. These points typically cast doubt upon or challenge the arguments that were made in the reading passage. Sometimes they may provide solutions to the problems posed in the reading.

Writing

The ideal response provides information on all the points and counterpoints that are given in the reading and the lecture. The summary should be about 150-225 words long although it may be longer. You should not give your opinion in the summary.

Question Types

1 Casting Doubt

- ◆ Summarize the points made in the lecture, being sure to explain how they cast doubt on specific points made in the reading passage.

- ◆ Summarize the points made in the lecture, being sure to explain how they challenge specific claims/arguments made in the reading passage.

   cf. This question type accounts for almost all of the questions that have been asked on the TOEFL iBT so far.

2 Problem-Solution

◆ Summarize the points made in the lecture, being sure to specifically explain how they answer the problems raised in the reading passage.

Useful Tips

1 Casting Doubt

You should mention all three points and counterpoints. You should relate each point and its counterpoint one at a time and provide the reasons why each counterpoint disagrees with the point in the reading passage.

2 Problem-Solution

You should note the individual solutions that the lecture provides for each problem. The professor will mention why each solution will work. You should be sure to include the reasons for these solutions in your response.

Key Strategies

1 Note Taking & Outlining

◆ Take notes on each point in the reading passage and the listening lecture.

◆ Focus on the main ideas, not the minor ones.

◆ Create an outline to show how every point and counterpoint relate to each other.

2 Paraphrasing & Summarizing

◆ Do not repeat the words in the reading passage exactly as they are written.

◆ Paraphrase the sentences from the reading passage and the listening lecture.

◆ Summarize the reading passage and the listening lecture in your own words.

3 Synthesizing & Organizing

◆ Recognize how the points and the counterpoints are related to one another.

◆ Be sure to mention all three of the points and counterpoints in your response.

◆ Organize your response by including an introduction and, when appropriate, a short conclusion.

4 Writing & Checking

◆ Write your response from the notes and outline that you wrote.

◆ Be sure to include an introduction, a body, and a conclusion. However, the conclusion is optional.

◆ Check over your writing to make sure that you did not make any mistakes.

Directions Now you will see the reading passage for 3 minutes. Remember that it will be available to you again while you are writing. Immediately after the reading time ends, the lecture will begin, so keep your headset on until the lecture has ended.

Reading

The golden barrel cactus is native to the deserts of Mexico and other places in Central America. Interestingly, this cactus is also found in some countries in Africa. How the cactus arrived there is a mystery some people have tried to explain.

This cactus can grow more than one meter in height and produces flowers at times. These flowers then produce seeds, which some birds eat. Some experts believe that a long time ago, migratory birds ate these seeds and then flew across the Atlantic Ocean. Then, the birds defecated the seeds, which grew into cacti in their new habitat. The cattle egret is one such bird capable of flying long distances and may have brought the cactus to Africa.

Another theory is related to continental drift. This is the theory that the Earth's continents were once united in a supercontinent called Pangaea. At that time, Africa was connected to parts of Central America. Then, it would have been easy for the cacti to move from Central America to Africa. Over a period of millions of years, Pangaea slowly broke apart. Then, the continents moved into the positions they currently occupy.

Listening

Now listen to part of a lecture on the topic you just read about.

Script

01-01

M Professor: Most of you should be familiar with the golden barrel cactus. It's a common cactus native to Mexico and Central America. It can also be found growing in various regions in Africa, including in South Africa. Some scientists believe they know how it got to Africa, but their theories all have problems.

The theory many botanists subscribe to is that birds such as the cattle egret ate cactus seeds. Then, they flew across the Atlantic Ocean and deposited the seeds in Africa. Well . . . the cattle egret is capable of migrating vast distances. But there's a problem. You see, uh, the cattle egret is carnivorous. It mostly eats insects but will eat other small animals. It does not, however, eat the seeds of cacti.

Other scientists have proposed that the cactus made it to Africa millions of years ago when the continents were all united. I find that a creative theory. But let me tell you what's wrong with it. Pangaea began to break apart about 200 million years ago. Various scientific tests have shown that the golden barrel cactus isn't nearly that old. In fact, it first appeared many millions of years after Pangaea split up.

Directions You have 20 minutes to plan and write your response. Your response will be judged on the basis of the quality of your writing and on how well your response presents the points in the lecture and their relationship to the reading passage. Typically, an effective response will be 150 to 225 words.

 Q Summarize the points made in the lecture, being sure to explain how they challenge specific claims made in the reading passage.

Sample Response

(Introductory sentence) The author of the reading passage provides two possible ways that the golden barrel cactus migrated from Mexico to Africa. (Topic sentence) However, the professor challenges both theories in his lecture.

(Refutation 1) First, the professor focuses on the notion that migratory birds such as the cattle egret crossed the Atlantic after eating cactus seeds. Then, they deposited them in Africa when they defecated. (Relation 1) While the author of the reading passage believes that happened, the professor mentions that the cattle egret does not eat cactus seeds. It could have flown across the Atlantic Ocean, but it never ate any seeds.

(Relation 2) Second, the professor disregards the theory about continental drift in the reading passage. According to it, Central America and Africa were once connected when Pangaea existed. (Refutation 2) The professor points out that scientific studies show that the golden barrel cactus did not exist until after Pangaea broke apart. As a result, this theory is also incorrect.

(Conclusion) The professor therefore challenges the two claims made in the reading passage.

Exercise Read, listen, and answer the question following each step.

Reading Read the following passage and take notes.

Nowadays, many people enjoy reading books on electronic devices or use apps to read on their computers. People often choose to read e-books because of their various advantages.

One benefit is cost. The prices of paper books have steadily climbed over the years. This makes it difficult for people to read many books. E-books, however, tend to cost half the price of paper books and can be even cheaper at times. It is even possible for people to acquire e-books of works whose copyrights have expired for free. In addition, most apps for reading e-books on computers are free to download. As a result, people spend much less on e-books than on paper books.

A second advantage is that e-books are better for the environment than paper books. Paper is made from wood pulp, which comes from trees. Cutting down trees, especially in large numbers, is harmful to the environment. Trees are essential for numerous ecosystems. They also provide oxygen for living organisms while removing carbon dioxide from the atmosphere. The more paper books people read, the more harm they do to the environment. E-books, however, cause no harm at all, so they can help preserve environments worldwide.

📖 Words & Phrases

device n a piece of machinery
advantage n a benefit
steadily adv constantly; regularly
climb v to go up; to rise
copyright n the legal right to sell, make, or use something
expire v to come to an end

wood pulp n material from trees that is treated with chemicals and used to make paper
essential adj necessary; needed
ecosystem n all of the organic and inorganic things in a region
organism n any living creature

✎ Note Taking

E-Books – Better than Paper Books

1   Cost [1)]_____ or less

  • Can acquire free e-books → books whose copyrights have expired
  • [2)]_____ free to download
  • Spend less on e-books than on paper books

2   Better for the environment than paper books
  • [3)]_____ to make paper books → harms environment
  • E-books = cause [4)]_____ → preserve environment worldwide

Listen to a lecture on the topic you just read about and take notes.

Note Taking

Paper Books – Not Worse than E-Books

01-02

1   Are many sources of [1)] _____

- Used bookstores, online auction sites, and libraries
- Must purchase e-book reader or computer = expensive
- Pay fee to [2)] _____

2   Paper books don't harm environment

- Paper = [3)] _____ → millions of trees planted each year
- E-book readers and computers cause pollution → parts not [4)] _____

Words & Phrases

popularity (n) the quality or state of being liked by others
proponent (n) a supporter of something
source (n) a person or place that supplies something
fee (n) a sum of money charged for a service
update (v) to bring up to date; to get a new version of something
renewable resource (n) a natural source of wealth or something useful that can be used again repeatedly

replace (v) to take the place of
pollution (n) the act of making an environment dirty or unclean
recycle (v) to use something again
discard (v) to throw away

Comparing the Points   Complete the main points from both notes as complete sentences.

E-Books vs. Paper Books

Reading (Main Points)	Listening (Main Points)
E-books cost much less than paper books and can sometimes be acquired for _____ . In addition, people can _____ apps for e-readers for free.	Used bookstores and online _____ provide paper books for cheap prices, and libraries have free books. E-book readers and computers are _____ , and upgrading apps requires a fee.
E-books also are not bad for the environment like paper books. _____ are cut down to make paper books, and cutting them down hurts numerous _____ .	Paper books are made from trees, which are _____ , so that hurts the environment. E-book readers and computers cause _____ when people just discard them.

Paraphrasing & Summarizing

A The following pairs of sentences are based on the reading. Complete each paraphrase by filling in the blanks with appropriate words or phrases. Then, complete the following summary.

1 Nowadays, many people enjoy reading books on electronic devices or use apps to read on their computers.

→ _____ use electronic devices or apps to

_____ .

2 E-books, however, tend to cost half the price of paper books and can be even cheaper at times.

→ E-books cost at least _____ than e-books and

_____ .

3 In addition, most apps for reading e-books on computers are free to download.

→ It _____ to download apps to read e-books

_____ .

4 Cutting down trees, especially in large numbers, is harmful to the environment.

→ It _____ when people _____ many

trees.

5 The more paper books people read, the more harm they do to the environment.

→ If people read _____ , they _____

a lot.

✎ Summary

Lots of people read e-books these days because of _____ . For instance, they are cheaper than paper books. Sometimes people can _____ for free. They also usually do not _____ to read e-books on computers. E-books are also _____ than paper books. Paper books require _____ to be cut down. This hurts the environment. E-books, meanwhile, do not hurt the environment at all.

B The following pairs of sentences are based on the listening. Complete each paraphrase by filling in the blanks with appropriate words or phrases. Then, complete the following summary.

1 Proponents of e-books claim they have multiple advantages over paper books.

→ _____ believe they _____ than paper books.

2 But remember that there are many sources of cheap paper books, including used bookstores and online auction sites.

→ Used bookstores and websites can _____ with

_____ .

3 When you add everything up, I don't think e-books actually are cheaper than paper books.

→ _____ , paper books are _____ than e-books.

4 Each year in many countries, millions of trees are planted to replace those that are cut down.

→ _____ are planted each year _____ the ones chopped down.

5 After all, many of their parts cannot be recycled, so people discard them in landfills after finishing using them.

→ People _____ because it _____ to recycle many of their parts.

✏ **Summary**

It is possible to get _____ in some places. People can get them for free at libraries, too. Buying an _____ or computer is expensive. And people might have to pay _____ e-book readers. So paper books are cheaper than e-books. Paper books are made from trees, but people _____ to replace the ones cut down. In addition, people usually throw away their e-book readers and computers, so this _____ .

The following sentences are some important points from both the reading and the listening. Combine each pair of sentences to create your own sentence by using the given patterns.

1   **Reading**   E-books, however, tend to cost half the price of paper books and can be even cheaper at times.

     Listening   But remember that there are many sources of cheap paper books, including used bookstores and online auction sites.

     Combine   The reading passage points out that _____

_____ ,

but the professor remarks that _____

_____ .

2   **Reading**   In addition, most apps for reading e-books on computers are free to download.

     Listening   You might also have to pay a fee to update your e-book reader.

     Combine   The author notes that _____

_____ ,

but the professor declares that _____

_____ .

3   **Reading**   Cutting down trees, especially in large numbers, is harmful to the environment.

     Listening   Each year in many countries, millions of trees are planted to replace those that are cut down.

     Combine   Whereas the reading passage claims that _____

_____ ,

the professor says that _____

_____ .

4   **Reading**   E-books, however, cause no harm at all, so they can help preserve environments worldwide.

     Listening   And please be aware that e-book readers and computers cause pollution.

     Combine   While the author claims that _____

_____ ,

the professor states that _____

_____ .

Organization   Review the notes from the reading and the listening. Complete the following chart with complete sentences.

Introduction	1 The lecture and the reading passage both _____ _____ . 2 The reading passage claims _____ , but the professor _____ .
Body 1	3 First, the professor points out _____ _____ . 4 This goes against the claim in the reading passage that _____ _____ . 5 While the reading passage states that _____ _____ , the professor remarks that _____ . 6 She also says _____ _____ .
Body 2	7 Second, the professor disagrees with the argument in the reading passage that _____ . 8 The reading passage claims that _____ , but the professor mentions that _____ . 9 She also notes that _____ _____ .
Conclusion (Optional)	10 In conclusion, the professor feels that _____ _____ .

Reading

Nowadays, many people enjoy reading books on electronic devices or use apps to read on their computers. People often choose to read e-books because of their various advantages.

One benefit is cost. The prices of paper books have steadily climbed over the years. This makes it difficult for people to read many books. E-books, however, tend to cost half the price of paper books and can be even cheaper at times. It is even possible for people to acquire e-books of works whose copyrights have expired for free. In addition, most apps for reading e-books on computers are free to download. As a result, people spend much less on e-books than on paper books.

A second advantage is that e-books are better for the environment than paper books. Paper is made from wood pulp, which comes from trees. Cutting down trees, especially in large numbers, is harmful to the environment. Trees are essential for numerous ecosystems. They also provide oxygen for living organisms while removing carbon dioxide from the atmosphere. The more paper books people read, the more harm they do to the environment. E-books, however, cause no harm at all, so they can help preserve environments worldwide.

Listening

✏ Note Taking

01-02

Q Summarize the points made in the lecture, being sure to explain how they cast doubt on specific points made in the reading passage.

Self-Evaluation Check your response by answering the following questions.

	Yes	No
1 Are all the important points from the lecture presented accurately?	☐	☐
2 Is the information from the lecture appropriately related to the reading?	☐	☐
3 Is the response well organized?	☐	☐
4 Are all the sentences grammatically correct?	☐	☐
5 Are all the words spelled correctly?	☐	☐
6 Are all the punctuation marks used correctly?	☐	☐

Exercise Read, listen, and answer the question following each step.

Reading Read the following passage and take notes.

Around the world, sea turtle populations are in decline. Approximately 6.5 million of them remain, which is two-thirds less than a hundred years ago. In addition, three of the seven main species are considered endangered.

One major reason for the loss of sea turtles is due to them eating plastic, particularly plastic bags. The turtles believe the bags are jellyfish, so they consume the bags. The bags then get stuck in the turtles' stomachs. This makes the turtles feel full, so they stop eating and die soon afterward. A possible solution would be to ban plastic bag usage worldwide.

Another problem sea turtles face is fishing in areas where they live in great numbers. Turtles are often caught by accident in fishing nets and on hooks on longlines. In Indonesia, an estimated 5,000 turtles are killed on longline hooks annually. These fishermen are not actively targeting sea turtles. They are instead caught accidentally. One solution to this problem is to prohibit fishermen from fishing in areas with large sea turtle populations. They could also use nets that allow turtles to escape.

📖 Words & Phrases

decline (n) the act of going down or decreasing in number

approximately (adv) around; about

endangered (adj) of a species having low numbers and in danger of extinction

consume (v) to eat

stuck (adj) being unable to move

ban (v) to prohibit; not to allow something

longline (n) a fishing line that may be several kilometers long and have many hooks

target (v) to set as a goal

accidentally (adv) not on purpose

prohibit (v) to ban; not to allow something

✏ Note Taking

Sea Turtles – Two Ways to Help Them

1   Harmed by eating plastic, especially bags
   - 1) _____ and then feel full ➜ stop eating and then die
   - Ban 2) _____ worldwide ➜ solve problem

2   1,000s killed when caught by fishermen
   - Caught in fishing nets and on 3) _____
   - 4) _____ from fishing in some areas + use nets that let turtles escape

🖋 Note Taking

Sea Turtle Decline – No Long-Term Solution

01-03

1   Enormous ¹⁾ _____ in oceans

   • Ban on plastic isn't practical

   • ²⁾ _____ w/plastic ➜ need centuries for it to dissolve

2   Solutions involving fishermen won't work

   • ³⁾ _____ for livelihoods ➜ can't ban them from fishing in some areas

   • Nets w/escape routes = expensive + ⁴⁾ _____ = reduce number of fish caught

📖 Words & Phrases

shrink Ⓥ to become smaller
marine adj related to the sea
enormous adj very large; huge
propose Ⓥ to suggest
saturated adj being a mixture so full of something and unable to take in any more

dissolve Ⓥ to cause to break down and spread out
particle Ⓝ a tiny piece of something
livelihood Ⓝ a means of subsistence or support
reduce Ⓥ to make smaller in size, amount, or quantity
reluctant adj feeling hesitant or unwilling to do something

Comparing the Points   Complete the main points from both notes as complete sentences.

The Decline of Sea Turtle Populations

Reading (Main Points)	Listening (Main Points)
Sea turtles eat _____, which get stuck in their stomachs. The turtles feel full, so they _____ anymore and then die.	There is so much plastic in the oceans that _____ is not practical. Hundreds of years are required for the plastic to break down into _____.
Many turtles are accidentally caught in _____ or on longlines. Fishermen could be banned from fishing in areas with many turtles and could use nets that let _____.	Fishermen's livelihoods depend on their _____, so they cannot be stopped from fishing in some places. And nets that let turtles escape are _____ and also let fish escape, so fishermen will not use them.

Paraphrasing & Summarizing

A The following pairs of sentences are based on the reading. Complete each paraphrase by filling in the blanks with appropriate words or phrases. Then, complete the following summary.

1 Approximately 6.5 million of them remain, which is two-thirds less than a hundred years ago.

→ 6.5 million sea turtles remain, a _____ decline from _____ ago.

2 One major reason for the loss of sea turtles is due to them eating plastic, particularly plastic bags.

→ Sea turtles _____ because so many of them _____ plastic bags.

3 This makes the turtles feel full, so they stop eating and die soon afterward.

→ The turtles are _____, so they _____ and die.

4 Turtles are often caught by accident in fishing nets and on hooks on longlines.

→ Fishermen _____ catch turtles in nets and _____.

5 One solution to this problem is to prohibit fishermen from fishing in areas with large sea turtle populations.

→ Sea turtles _____ if fishermen are _____ in some places.

🖊 Summary

There has been a tremendous decline in the _____ in the past century. For one, the turtles eat plastic, especially bags. The bags get stuck _____, so the turtles feel full, stop eating, and die. Banning _____ could help the turtles. Fishermen also _____ in nets and on hooks. They could be banned from fishing in places with many turtles and could _____ that let turtles escape.

B The following pairs of sentences are based on the listening. Complete each paraphrase by filling in the blanks with appropriate words or phrases. Then, complete the following summary.

1 Sea turtles help maintain certain marine ecosystems, especially coral reefs.

→ Sea turtles _____ ocean ecosystems _____ coral reefs.

2 Some individuals have proposed banning the use of plastic products such as bags.

→ Some people believe _____ like bags should _____.

3 The oceans are so saturated with plastic that it would take centuries for all of it to dissolve into tiny particles.

→ _____ is in the oceans that it will not break down for _____.

4 There have been proposals to ban fishing in certain areas and to require nets that turtles can escape from.

→ _____ prohibiting fishing in some places and requiring _____.

5 The nets also let fish get out, which would reduce the number of fish fishermen catch.

→ Fish _____ from the nets, so fishermen would _____.

✏ **Summary**

There are no _____ to the decline in sea turtle numbers. Some people think _____ would help turtles. But the oceans already have _____. It will require centuries for the plastic in the oceans _____. Other people want to ban fishing in certain places and to require specialized nets. But the nets are expensive and _____, so fishermen will not use them.

The following sentences are some important points from both the reading and the listening. Combine each pair of sentences to create your own sentence by using the given patterns.

1 **Reading** One major reason for the loss of sea turtles is due to them eating plastic, particularly plastic bags.

     Listening There is an enormous amount of plastic in the oceans. It kills not only sea turtles but also many other sea creatures.

     Combine The author mentions that _____

_____ ,

and the professor says that _____

_____ .

2 **Reading** A possible solution would be to ban plastic bag usage worldwide.

     Listening The oceans are so saturated with plastic that it would take centuries for all of it to dissolve into tiny particles.

     Combine While the author of the reading passage suggests _____

_____ ,

the professor remarks that _____

_____ .

3 **Reading** One solution to this problem is to prohibit fishermen from fishing in areas with large sea turtle populations.

     Listening Most fishermen depend on their daily catches for their livelihoods.

     Combine Although the author wants to _____

_____ ,

the professor points out that _____

_____ .

4 **Reading** They could also use nets that allow turtles to escape.

     Listening The nets also let fish get out, which would reduce the number of fish fishermen catch.

     Combine The reading passage author believes _____

_____ ,

but the professor claims _____

_____ .

Organization Review the notes from the reading and the listening. Complete the following chart with complete sentences.

Introduction	1 The reading passage states it is possible to stop .... , but the professor ....
Body 1	2 First, the professor points out that there is already .... in the oceans.
	3 In fact, there is so much plastic that ....
	4 The professor therefore refutes the claim in the reading passage that ....
Body 2	5 Second, the professor discusses fishermen who ....
	6 He says banning them from fishing in some places will not work because ....
	7 He also remarks that fishermen will not buy nets that ....
	8 The nets are too expensive and ....
	9 In this way, he challenges the claim that forcing fishermen to act differently ....
Conclusion (Optional)	10 The professor uses these two arguments to prove ....

Reading

Around the world, sea turtle populations are in decline. Approximately 6.5 million of them remain, which is two-thirds less than a hundred years ago. In addition, three of the seven main species are considered endangered.

One major reason for the loss of sea turtles is due to them eating plastic, particularly plastic bags. The turtles believe the bags are jellyfish, so they consume the bags. The bags then get stuck in the turtles' stomachs. This makes the turtles feel full, so they stop eating and die soon afterward. A possible solution would be to ban plastic bag usage worldwide.

Another problem sea turtles face is fishing in areas where they live in great numbers. Turtles are often caught by accident in fishing nets and on hooks on longlines. In Indonesia, an estimated 5,000 turtles are killed on longline hooks annually. These fishermen are not actively targeting sea turtles. They are instead caught accidentally. One solution to this problem is to prohibit fishermen from fishing in areas with large sea turtle populations. They could also use nets that allow turtles to escape.

Listening

| ✏ Note Taking |

01-03

Q Summarize the points made in the lecture, being sure to explain how they challenge specific claims made in the reading passage.

Self-Evaluation Check your response by answering the following questions.

	Yes	No
1 Are all the important points from the lecture presented accurately?	☐	☐
2 Is the information from the lecture appropriately related to the reading?	☐	☐
3 Is the response well organized?	☐	☐
4 Are all the sentences grammatically correct?	☐	☐
5 Are all the words spelled correctly?	☐	☐
6 Are all the punctuation marks used correctly?	☐	☐

Exercise Read, listen, and answer the question following each step.

Reading Read the following passage and take notes.

A lie detector is a machine capable of showing if a person is lying. It measures a person's heart rate, blood pressure, and breathing patterns. Police often use it when questioning criminal suspects. However, courts sometimes do not accept the results as evidence. This may change in the future though.

People being questioned with a lie detector may find ways to control the results. They can learn to physically control their breathing and heart rate. New lie detectors, however, measure brain activity. When people lie, certain regions of the brain become more active. It is virtually impossible for people to control their brain activity. These new lie detectors can thus prevent people from hiding the truth by lying.

In many countries, lie detector results are not used as evidence in criminal cases. Real criminals may control their bodies while innocent people may produce guilty results. The reason is they are too nervous when taking the test. Lie detectors thus erroneously show them as lying even though they are telling the truth. New lie detectors measuring brain activity will reduce this problem. In the future, therefore, many courts will accept their results as evidence.

📖 Words & Phrases

lie v to make a false statement; not to tell the truth on purpose
heart rate n the rate that the heart beats
criminal adj relating to activities against the law
suspect n a person believed to have committed a crime
physically adv with respect to the body

measure v to determine an amount, degree, or length
virtually adv practically; nearly
evidence n proof
nervous adj overly concerned; timid; worried
erroneously adv mistakenly

✎ Note Taking

Lie Detectors – Will Be Used by Courts Soon

1 New lie detectors measure brain activity

- People can [1) _____] w/old lie detectors
- Virtually impossible to [2) _____] → new lie detectors prevent people from lying

2 Lie detector results not used in criminal trials

- Criminals control bodies, but innocent may [3) _____]
- New lie detectors will [4) _____] like that → may be accepted by courts

✎ Note Taking

New Lie Detectors – Are Beatable

01-04

1 People can control brain activity
- Brain mapped while in [1)] _____
- University study had people use mental defenses to hide lies
- Reduced detector's ability by [2)] _____

2 People's brains = different
- [3)] _____ may have different results for people
- [4)] _____ lie a lot → no unusual brain activity when tell falsehoods

📖 Words & Phrases

breakthrough (n) a sudden advance or development in knowledge or technology

unbeatable (adj) not able to be defeated or to lose

connect (v) to put two things together

sensor (n) a device that responds to physical stimulus

MRI machine (n) a device that produces images of the inside of the body

map (v) to make or draw a representation of something

hide (v) to keep secret; to put out of sight

standard (adj) normal; typical

seasoned (adj) experienced

falsehood (n) a lie

Comparing the Points   Complete the main points from both notes as complete sentences.

New Lie Detectors

Reading (Main Points)	Listening (Main Points)
People can control their breathing and _____ when they take lie detector tests. But new lie detectors measure _____, which people cannot control.	An _____ measures brain activity during the test. But a 2019 university study showed that people could use _____ to hide their lies effectively.
Criminals can control their bodies, but _____ may get nervous, so the lie detector shows they are lying. _____ will reduce the likelihood of this happening.	People have _____, so standard tests might not work for everyone. Seasoned criminals also lie so much that they show no _____ brain activity when they lie.

Paraphrasing & Summarizing

A The following pairs of sentences are based on the reading. Complete each paraphrase by filling in the blanks with appropriate words or phrases. Then, complete the following summary.

1 A lie detector is a machine capable of showing if a person is lying.

→ A lie detector is _____ that can _____.

2 People being questioned with a lie detector may find ways to control the results.

→ _____ can control the results of their

_____.

3 It is virtually impossible for people to control their brain activity.

→ _____ have _____ over their brain

activity.

4 Real criminals may control their bodies while innocent people may produce guilty results.

→ _____ might product _____ whereas

criminals can control their bodies.

5 Lie detectors thus erroneously show them as lying even though they are telling the truth.

→ _____, lie detectors show that _____

were telling lies.

✏ Summary

Lie detector results are not accepted in most courts. The reason is that some people can _____. But new lie detectors _____, which almost nobody can control. In addition, criminals can control their bodies while innocent people _____ during tests. This makes lie detectors have wrong results. _____ will reduce the likelihood of this happening though. As a result, courts will _____ in the future.

B The following pairs of sentences are based on the listening. Complete each paraphrase by filling in the blanks with appropriate words or phrases. Then, complete the following summary.

1 This breakthrough has led people to believe lie detectors are now unbeatable.

→ A _____ has made people think lie detectors

_____.

2 However, there's evidence that people can control their brain activity during tests.

→ Yet people _____ to be able to control their brains

_____.

3 They reduced the detector's ability to tell if they were lying by twenty percent.

→ The lie detector's _____ was lowered by

_____.

4 Some people may show brain activity when they lie whereas others may not.

→ _____ exhibit any brain activity when they

_____.

5 There's also evidence that seasoned criminals are so used to lying that there's no unusual brain activity when they tell falsehoods.

→ People _____ lie so much that their brains show

_____ when they lie.

✏ Summary

Some people think that new lie detectors _____, but they are wrong. An MRI machine _____ during tests. However, a 2019 university study showed that people could use mental defenses effectively to _____. In addition, people's brains are different, so some may show _____ when they lie. Criminals _____ that they exhibit no special brain activity, too. So the results may never be used in courts.

The following sentences are some important points from both the reading and the listening. Combine each pair of sentences to create your own sentence by using the given patterns.

1 **Reading**   It is virtually impossible for people to control their brain activity.

   Listening   However, there's evidence that people can control their brain activity during tests.

   Combine   While the reading passage argues that .... ,

   the professor argues that ....

2 **Reading**   These new lie detectors can thus prevent people from hiding the truth by lying.

   Listening   Subjects tested utilized mental defenses to hide their lies.

   Combine   In contrast to the claim that .... ,

   the professor shows that ....

3 **Reading**   Real criminals may control their bodies while innocent people may produce guilty results.

   Listening   A standard test of the brain for lying may not work on everyone.

   Combine   The author writes that .... ,

   but the professor states that ....

4 **Reading**   In the future, therefore, many courts will accept their results as evidence.

   Listening   As a result, the results are not yet being used as evidence by courts . . . and maybe they never will be.

   Combine   Whereas the author of the reading passage believes .... ,

   the professor thinks ....

Organization   Review the notes from the reading and the listening. Complete the following chart with complete sentences.

Introduction	**1** In the reading passage, the writer argues that new lie detectors _____ _____. **2** However, the professor disagrees with _____ _____.
Body 1	**3** The professor first discusses how the new lie detector _____ _____. **4** He then mentions a university study in which people _____ _____. **5** This made the new lie detectors _____ _____. **6** He therefore shows that the argument in the reading passage _____ _____.
Body 2	**7** Next, the professor points out that everyone's brain is different, so _____ _____. **8** He also remarks that criminals lie so much that _____ _____. **9** In this way, he shows that _____ _____.
Conclusion (Optional)	**10** The professor therefore _____ _____ made in the reading passage.

Reading

A lie detector is a machine capable of showing if a person is lying. It measures a person's heart rate, blood pressure, and breathing patterns. Police often use it when questioning criminal suspects. However, courts often do not accept the results as evidence. This may change in the future though.

People being questioned with a lie detector may find ways to control the results. They can learn to physically control their breathing and heart rate. New lie detectors, however, measure brain activity. When people lie, certain regions of the brain become more active. It is virtually impossible for people to control their brain activity. These new lie detectors can thus prevent people from hiding the truth by lying.

In many countries, lie detector results are not used as evidence in criminal cases. Real criminals may control their bodies while innocent people may produce guilty results. The reason is they are too nervous when taking the test. Lie detectors thus erroneously show them as lying even though they are telling the truth. New lie detectors measuring brain activity will reduce this problem. In the future, therefore, many courts will accept their results as evidence.

Listening

✎ Note Taking

01-04

Q Summarize the points made in the lecture, being sure to explain how they cast doubt on specific points made in the reading passage.

_____

_____

_____

_____

_____

_____

_____

_____

_____

_____

_____

_____

_____

_____

_____

_____

_____

_____

Self-Evaluation Check your response by answering the following questions.

	Yes	No
1 Are all the important points from the lecture presented accurately?	☐	☐
2 Is the information from the lecture appropriately related to the reading?	☐	☐
3 Is the response well organized?	☐	☐
4 Are all the sentences grammatically correct?	☐	☐
5 Are all the words spelled correctly?	☐	☐
6 Are all the punctuation marks used correctly?	☐	☐

Exercise Read, listen, and answer the question following each step.

Reading Read the following passage and take notes.

A mission to Mars is currently being planned by NASA, the American space agency. One major concern about the mission is where to land on Mars. Two locations have been suggested: the equator or one of the poles. The better choice would be somewhere near the Martian equator.

Any long-term mission to Mars must find water to be successful. After all, water is essential to human survival and to grow food. Scientists have pinpointed eight potential landing sites near the equator. These sites are good because they show evidence of having water beneath the surface. By drilling into the ground, astronauts will be able to pump out water.

The equator is also warmer than any other location on Mars. Temperatures there can reach as high as twenty degrees Celsius in summer. On the contrary, places near the poles have recorded temperatures as low as minus one hundred degrees Celsius. The equator also has longer daytime hours and more sunlight than the poles. Any mission to Mars would rely on solar power to operate machinery. The poles would receive limited amounts of sunlight all day, thereby making it difficult to produce solar power.

📖 Words & Phrases

mission (n) a specific task; a group of people sent to another place with a certain goal
concern (n) a worry
pole (n) the northernmost or southernmost place on a sphere, such as a planet or moon
essential (adj) very important; necessary
pinpoint (v) to locate with great accuracy

potential (adj) being highly possible
evidence (n) proof; something that shows proof
drill (v) to make a hole into
temperature (n) the degree of hotness or coldness in a place
on the contrary (phr) however; in contrast

✏ Note Taking

Mars Mission – Should Visit the Equator

1 Must have water to survive

• Eight 1) _____ near equator

• Have evidence of water 2) _____ → can drill down and pump out water

2 Warmer temperatures at equator

• Can be 3) _____ at equator but minus 100 at poles

• More sunlight at equator → will use 4) _____ to run machinery

---

✏ Note Taking

Mars Mission – Should Land at Pole

1 1) .... w/frozen water at poles

   • 2) .... for astronauts

   • Not easy to obtain water at equator

2 3) .... at equator

   • Ranges from warm to very cold ➜ hard on machinery, so it will 4) ....

   • Use nuclear generator to produce power at pole

01-05

📖 Words & Phrases

dream v to imagine; to consider the possibility of

establish v to found; to make; to create

permanent adj continuing for a long time

base n a center of operations

consideration n something that must be taken into account

guarantee n an assurance

fluctuation n the act of moving up and down in level

expand v to become greater in size, quantity, or amount

contract v to become smaller in size, quantity, or amount

generator n a machine that creates electricity

Comparing the Points   Complete the main points from both notes as complete sentences.

Mars Mission: Equator vs. Pole

Reading (Main Points)	Listening (Main Points)
There are eight potential sites to land at .... They should have water beneath the surface that astronauts can drill down to	There is .... at the permanent ice caps at the poles, which will give astronauts a long-term water supply. At the equator, astronauts might .... but not find any water.
The equator can get as warm as twenty degrees Celsius, making it much warmer than .... It has more access to ...., so astronauts can use solar power to operate machinery.	At the equator, there are temperature fluctuations, which will be .... and make it break down. At a pole, nuclear energy could be used to ....

A The following pairs of sentences are based on the reading. Complete each paraphrase by filling in the blanks with appropriate words or phrases. Then, complete the following summary.

1 A mission to Mars is currently being planned by NASA, the American space agency.

→ NASA _____ to send _____ to Mars.

2 These sites are good because they show evidence of having water beneath the surface.

→ The sites _____ since they are believed to have

_____.

3 By drilling into the ground, astronauts will be able to pump out water.

→ Astronauts can _____ the ground and

_____ the water.

4 On the contrary, places near the poles have recorded temperatures as low as minus one hundred degrees Celsius.

→ However, _____ can get _____ at the Martian poles.

5 The poles would receive limited amounts of sunlight all day, thereby making it difficult to produce solar power.

→ There is _____ at the poles, so _____ can be produced.

Summary

NASA is planning to send astronauts to Mars and should land _____. There are eight spots around the equator that should have _____. Astronauts can drill into the ground and then _____ to survive. The temperature at the equator can be twenty degrees Celsius whereas it is extremely cold at the poles. The equator also gets _____, so it will be possible to operate machinery with _____.

B The following pairs of sentences are based on the listening. Complete each paraphrase by filling in the blanks with appropriate words or phrases. Then, complete the following summary.

1 Members of the space community have long dreamed of establishing a permanent base on Mars.

→ People _____ have wanted to visit Mars _____ .

2 The Martian north and south poles both have permanent ice caps of frozen water on the surface.

→ There is _____ at the permanent ice caps at both of _____ .

3 While the equator has water, it will not be easy to obtain there.

→ _____ the equator has water, _____ will be hard.

4 The temperature can range from twenty degrees Celsius in the day to far into the negatives at night.

→ The _____ is twenty degrees Celsius while the low is _____ .

5 Yet a Mars base at a pole could use a nuclear generator to produce all the power it needs.

→ Astronauts at the poles could use _____ for their _____ .

✏️ **Summary**

A _____ should visit one of the poles. Astronauts can get long-term access to water at the _____ there. There is water at the equator, but getting it _____ . Astronauts might dig but _____ . The temperature fluctuates too much at the equator. That will make equipment _____ and then break down. Astronauts at a pole can generate electricity by using nuclear power.

The following sentences are some important points from both the reading and the listening. Combine each pair of sentences to create your own sentence by using the given patterns.

1 **Reading** These sites are good because they show evidence of having water beneath the surface.

   Listening The Martian north and south poles both have permanent ice caps of frozen water on the surface.

   Combine Although the author states that _____

   _____ ,

   the professor points out _____

   _____ .

2 **Reading** By drilling into the ground, astronauts will be able to pump out water.

   Listening There's also no guarantee they will find water where they land at the equator.

   Combine While the reading passage notes that _____

   _____ ,

   the professor says that _____

   _____ .

3 **Reading** Temperatures there can reach as high as twenty degrees Celsius in summer.

   Listening The temperature can range from twenty degrees Celsius in the day to far into the negatives at night.

   Combine Both the reading passage and the professor acknowledge _____

   _____ ,

   but the professor adds that _____

   _____ .

4 **Reading** The poles would receive limited amounts of sunlight all day, thereby making it difficult to produce solar power.

   Listening Yet a Mars base at a pole could use a nuclear generator to produce all the power it needs.

   Combine Whereas the author of the reading passage mentions that _____

   _____ ,

   the professor argues in favor of _____

   _____ .

Organization   Review the notes from the reading and the listening. Complete the following chart with complete sentences.

Introduction	1 The reading passage and the lecture are both about .... 2 However, the professor disagrees with ....
Body 1	3 To begin with, the professor states that the north and south poles of Mars .... 4 Then, she says that water at the equator is underground, which .... 5 This challenges the argument made in the reading passage that ....
Body 2	6 After that, the professor discusses .... 7 The temperature at the poles is constant, so .... 8 The temperature at the equator fluctuates too much, which .... 9 The professor therefore contradicts the argument that ....
Conclusion (Optional)	10 In her lecture, the professor .... made in the reading passage.

Reading

A mission to Mars is currently being planned by NASA, the American space agency. One major concern about the mission is where to land on Mars. Two locations have been suggested: the equator or one of the poles. The better choice would be somewhere near the Martian equator.

Any long-term mission to Mars must find water to be successful. After all, water is essential to human survival and to grow food. Scientists have pinpointed eight potential landing sites near the equator. These sites are good because they show evidence of having water beneath the surface. By drilling into the ground, astronauts will be able to pump out water.

The equator is also warmer than any other location on Mars. Temperatures there can reach as high as twenty degrees Celsius in summer. On the contrary, places near the poles have recorded temperatures as low as minus one hundred degrees Celsius. The equator also has longer daytime hours and more sunlight than the poles. Any mission to Mars would rely on solar power to operate machinery. The poles would receive limited amounts of sunlight all day, thereby making it difficult to produce solar power.

Listening

✎ Note Taking

01-05

Q Summarize the points made in the lecture, being sure to explain how they challenge specific arguments made in the reading passage.

		Yes	No
1	Are all the important points from the lecture presented accurately?	☐	☐
2	Is the information from the lecture appropriately related to the reading?	☐	☐
3	Is the response well organized?	☐	☐
4	Are all the sentences grammatically correct?	☐	☐
5	Are all the words spelled correctly?	☐	☐
6	Are all the punctuation marks used correctly?	☐	☐

Exercise Read, listen, and answer the question following each step.

Reading Read the following passage and take notes.

There is an ongoing debate about teaching music to elementary school students. While some people believe it is necessary, others do not. Overall, there are more disadvantages to teaching music than advantages.

For instance, in order properly to teach music, a lot of class time is required. This time, however, could be used to study other more vital skills, such as math and languages. Music is a skill which many people never use again after they graduate. On the other hand, knowledge gained in math, reading, science, and foreign language classes will benefit students for their entire lives. Therefore, learning music is a waste of valuable time for students.

The cost is another detriment to teaching music. Regular elementary school teachers instruct students in multiple courses. But they cannot teach music since it requires special skills. So schools must hire full-time music teachers. Due to the extra expense, teaching music is not particularly cost effective. Musical instruments can also be costly. Some cost more than a thousand dollars. Students' parents are expected to pay for these instruments, yet many cannot afford them. This makes learning music too expensive for elementary school students.

📖 Words & Phrases

ongoing adj happening at the present time
debate n a discussion between two or more people with different opinions
properly adv correctly
vital adj important
graduate v to complete a course of study at a school
benefit v to help

waste n the act of spending time or money poorly
detriment n something that causes damage or harm
cost effective adj producing good results for a small amount of money
afford v to have enough money to pay for a good or service

✏ Note Taking

Elementary Schools Should Teach Music

1 Much time required to teach music

- Could be used for other skills ➜ math and languages
- Most won't use music skills [1] ....
- Will use [2] ...., and languages skills for entire lives

2 Cost of teaching music = too high

- Schools hire [3] ....
- [4] .... expensive ➜ students' parents often can't afford

🖉 Note Taking

Elementary School Students Learning English – Wonderful Idea

01 - 06

1 Benefit from studying music at young age

- Reading [1)]_____ + playing instruments = long-term benefits
- Recognize patterns → useful for language and math
- Can [2)]_____ in other subjects

2 Can offset expensive prices of instruments

- Hire part-time or [3)]_____ + parents volunteer
- Rent [4)]_____ + some families already have at home

📖 Words & Phrases

oppose v to be against

sheet music n musical notes that are written on paper

pattern n a particular arrangement of parts

reinforce v to make stronger

lifetime n the time from one's birth to death

offset v to make up for; to serve as a counterbalance

retired adj no longer working, often due to age

volunteer v to work for no money

rent v to pay money to use something for a certain amount of time

outright adv completely; in entirety

Comparing the Points Complete the main points from both notes as complete sentences.

Teaching Music to Elementary School Students

Reading (Main Points)	Listening (Main Points)
It takes _____ to teach music, but that time could be used for other subjects, such as math and languages. In addition, many students do not use their music skills after they graduate, but they use _____ learned in other classes.	People can _____ from learning to read sheet music and to play musical instruments at a young age. They also learn to recognize patterns and _____ their skills in various subjects.
Schools must hire full-time music teachers, which is not _____. Students also need musical instruments, but they are expensive, so many parents cannot _____ them.	Schools can hire part-time or retired music teachers or get _____ to volunteer. Families can also _____ instruments or use ones that they already have.

Paraphrasing & Summarizing

A **The following pairs of sentences are based on the reading. Complete each paraphrase by filling in the blanks with appropriate words or phrases. Then, complete the following summary.**

1 Overall, there are more disadvantages to teaching music than advantages.

→ There are more ______________________ than ______________________ to teaching music.

2 Music is a skill which many people never use again after they graduate.

→ Most people will not use their ______________________ after they ______________________.

3 On the other hand, knowledge gained in math, reading, science, and foreign language classes will benefit students for their entire lives.

→ However, students will use the knowledge they learn in ______________________ for as long as ______________________.

4 Regular elementary school teachers instruct students in multiple courses.

→ Children's ______________________ teach many ______________________.

5 Students' parents are expected to pay for these instruments, yet many cannot afford them.

→ Students' parents ______________________ for the instruments but do not ______________________.

Summary

There are more ______________________ than advantages to teaching elementary school students music. For instance, most students ______________________ after they finish school. But they use skills learned in other classes for the rest of their lives. This makes learning music a ______________________. Schools also ______________________ full-time music teachers, which can be expensive. And ______________________ do not have enough money to buy musical instruments for their children.

B The following pairs of sentences are based on the listening. Complete each paraphrase by filling in the blanks with appropriate words or phrases. Then, complete the following summary.

1 It's unfortunate that so many people are opposed to elementary school students learning music.

→ It is _____ people do not want young students to

_____ .

2 Learning how to make music by reading sheet music and playing instruments has numerous long-term benefits.

→ There are _____ to learn to read music and to play music.

3 By learning music, students can reinforce their skills in other subjects.

→ Students can _____ to make other skills

_____ .

4 Schools can hire part-time or retired music teachers instead of full-time ones.

→ Schools can _____ part-time teachers or ones that

_____ .

5 It's also cheap simply to rent musical instruments rather than to buy them outright.

→ _____ is cheaper than paying to

_____ .

✏️ **Summary**

Teaching music to elementary school students is a _____ . Students can gain by learning to read _____ and to play instruments. They can also use music to _____ they have in other subjects. Schools can hire part-time or retired teachers or have parents with musical talents volunteer instead of hiring expensive _____ . They can also save money by renting instruments or by _____ they have at their homes.

The following sentences are some important points from both the reading and the listening. Combine each pair of sentences to create your own sentence by using the given patterns.

1   **Reading**   Music is a skill which many people never use again after they graduate.

   Listening   Learning how to make music by reading sheet music and playing instruments has numerous long-term benefits.

   Combine   Whereas the reading passage claims _____

   _____ ,

   the professor states that _____

   _____ .

2   **Reading**   Therefore, learning music is a waste of valuable time for students.

   Listening   By learning music, students can reinforce their skills in other subjects.

   Combine   The reading passage argues that _____

   _____ ,

   but the professor states that _____

   _____ .

3   **Reading**   So schools must hire full-time music teachers.

   Listening   Schools can hire part-time or retired music teachers instead of full-time ones.

   Combine   Although the author of the reading passage believes _____

   _____ ,

   the professor remarks that _____

   _____ .

4   **Reading**   Students' parents are expected to pay for these instruments, yet many cannot afford them.

   Listening   It's also cheap simply to rent musical instruments rather than to buy them outright.

   Combine   The reading passage mentions that _____

   _____ ,

   yet the professor points out that _____

   _____ .

Review the notes from the reading and the litsening. Complete the following chart with complete sentences.

Introduction	1 Both the lecture and the reading passage are concerned about ....
Body 1	2 The professor supports this activity by pointing out .... 3 She mentions that .... 4 She therefore casts doubt on the claim in the reading passage that ....
Body 2	5 The professor then discusses .... 6 Instead of ...., she wants to .... 7 She also notes that .... 8 Then, she says that .... 9 She adds that ....
Conclusion (Optional)	10 By bringing up those points, the professor ....

Reading

There is an ongoing debate about teaching music to elementary school students. While some people believe it is necessary, others do not. Overall, there are more disadvantages to teaching music than advantages.

For instance, in order properly to teach music, a lot of class time is required. This time, however, could be used to study other more vital skills, such as math and languages. Music is a skill which many people never use again after they graduate. On the other hand, knowledge gained in math, reading, science, and foreign language classes will benefit students for their entire lives. Therefore, learning music is a waste of valuable time for students.

The cost is another detriment to teaching music. Regular elementary school teachers instruct students in multiple courses. But they cannot teach music since it requires special skills. So schools must hire full-time music teachers. Due to the extra expense, teaching music is not particularly cost effective. Musical instruments can also be costly. Some cost more than a thousand dollars. Students' parents are expected to pay for these instruments, yet many cannot afford them. This makes learning music too expensive for elementary school students.

Listening

✎ Note Taking

01-06

Q Summarize the points made in the lecture, being sure to explain how they cast doubt on specific points made in the reading passage.

_____

_____

_____

_____

_____

_____

_____

_____

_____

_____

_____

_____

_____

_____

_____

_____

_____

_____

Self-Evaluation Check your response by answering the following questions.

	Yes	No
1 Are all the important points from the lecture presented accurately?	☐	☐
2 Is the information from the lecture appropriately related to the reading?	☐	☐
3 Is the response well organized?	☐	☐
4 Are all the sentences grammatically correct?	☐	☐
5 Are all the words spelled correctly?	☐	☐
6 Are all the punctuation marks used correctly?	☐	☐

Exercise Read, listen, and answer the question following each step.

Reading Read the following passage and take notes.

The bald cypress is a tree that typically grows in swamps and other wetlands. It is noted for its distinct roots, which grow vertically out of the water and are sometimes called knees. These roots have two primary functions: to absorb oxygen and to anchor the tree to the ground.

Plants require oxygen in order to undergo photosynthesis to make food. Plants in wetlands such as swamps often have roots underwater, which makes it difficult to absorb oxygen from the air. Bald cypress roots, however, grow above the waterline. This allows the tree more easily to absorb oxygen from the air. Since it takes in more oxygen, it grows taller and larger than many other wetland trees.

The bald cypress also needs to anchor itself to the soil. Wetlands have loose soil because they are usually covered with water. By growing more roots, plants in wetlands are better able to anchor themselves to the ground. This keeps the tree from getting knocked over by high winds or flood conditions. The tree's roots also help absorb water from the wetlands, which makes the soil less loose. This, in turn, prevents soil erosion.

📖 Words & Phrases

swamp n an area of land partially or completely covered with water and thick vegetation
wetland n land that is often covered with a small amount of water and has moist ground
root n the part of the plant that grows underground and extracts water and nutrients from the soil
vertically adv in an upward direction
primary adj main; important

absorb v to take in, as in a liquid
photosynthesis n the process in which plants make sugar and oxygen from carbon dioxide and water
waterline n the line marking the level of the water in a river, ocean, lake, etc.
anchor v to hold firmly in place
soil erosion n the process in which soil is worn away, often by wind or water

---

✏️ Note Taking

Bald Cypress Tree Roots – 2 Primary Functions

1   Needs oxygen for [1] _____

   • Roots grow above [2] _____ → absorb oxygen more easily
   • Takes in more oxygen → grows bigger and taller than other trees

2   Needs to anchor itself to soil

   • Grows more roots → keeps from getting knocked over by [3] _____ and floods
   • Roots absorb more water → prevents [4] _____

Listen to a lecture on the topic you just read about and take notes.

✏ Note Taking

Bald Cypress Tree Roots – Problems with Claimed Functions

01-07

1 Vertical roots grow above water

- Compared bald cypress trees growing on dry land and in [1] _____
- No significantly higher [2] _____ in trees in wetlands

2 Roots that anchor tree to ground

- [3] _____ = grow above soil so don't anchor tree
- [4] _____ = grow underground and spread out → anchor tree to soil

📖 Words & Phrases

distinct adj unique
resemble v to look like
function n a use; a purpose
botanist n a scientist who studies plants
precisely adv exactly

comparison n the act of describing how two things are similar or different
significantly adv in an important manner
horizontal adj parallel to the ground
spread out v to move outward over a large area
stability n the state of being fixed or unmoving

Comparing the Points   Complete the main points from both notes as complete sentences.

Functions of Bald Cypress Tree Roots

Reading (Main Points)	Listening (Main Points)
Bald cypress roots grow above the waterline, so they can absorb more _____ for photosynthesis. Because they take in so much oxygen, they grow taller and larger than other _____ .	Bald cypress trees grow on _____ and in wetlands. A comparison of trees showed that ones growing in wetlands did not have _____ higher levels of oxygen.
Bald cypress tree roots grow above the ground, so they can _____ the tree to the ground better. Their roots _____ _____ , too, so they help prevent soil erosion.	The horizontal roots that grow above the soil do not act as _____ . The vertical roots that grow underground _____ , so they anchor the tree to the soil.

A The following pairs of sentences are based on the reading. Complete each paraphrase by filling in the blanks with appropriate words or phrases. Then, complete the following summary.

1 It is noted for its distinct roots, which grow vertically out of the water and are sometimes called knees.

→ The _____ are called knees and grow _____ out of the water.

2 Plants require oxygen in order to undergo photosynthesis to make food.

→ _____ by _____ during photosynthesis.

3 Since it takes in more oxygen, it grows taller and larger than many other wetland trees.

→ Because it _____, it is bigger than other trees _____.

4 By growing more roots, plants in wetlands are better able to anchor themselves to the ground.

→ Since they _____, wetland trees can _____ better.

5 The tree's roots also help absorb water from the wetlands, which makes the soil less loose.

→ The soil is _____ because the roots _____ from the wetlands.

✎ **Summary**

The bald cypress tree has distinct roots growing out of the ground and called _____.
These roots help the tree _____ since they absorb so much oxygen. They
also grow _____ than other trees in wetlands. The roots of the tree help
anchor it to the soil, so it does not get _____ by the wind or floods. The
roots also absorb water, so they _____.

B The following pairs of sentences are based on the listening. Complete each paraphrase by filling in the blanks with appropriate words or phrases. Then, complete the following summary.

1 These roots are called knees because they resemble human knees.

→ The roots are _____ knees since that is what they
_____.

2 Some botanists claim the vertical roots enable the tree to absorb more oxygen from the air than other trees.

→ Plant _____ say vertical roots let the tree
_____ more oxygen than other trees.

3 You see, uh, some bald cypress trees grow on dry land and have no aboveground roots.

→ Bald cypress trees _____ on dry land do not have roots
_____.

4 However, these roots grow up and above the soil and are not actually in the ground beneath the water.

→ The roots do not go _____ because they are growing
_____.

5 Perhaps the vertical roots provide better stability for the horizontal roots, but more studies are needed to determine that.

→ The vertical roots _____ the horizontal ones more stable, but this
needs to _____ more.

✐ **Summary**

The bald cypress tree has aboveground roots _____. Botanists say that
the roots let the tree absorb more oxygen than _____. But a comparison of
trees growing in water and on dry land showed no significant difference in _____
_____. In addition, the _____ growing above the ground do not
anchor the tree in the soil. The horizontal roots growing in the soil do, however, _____
_____.

The following sentences are some important points from both the reading and the listening. Combine each pair of sentences to create your own sentence by using the given patterns.

1 **Reading** This allows the tree more easily to absorb oxygen from the air.

Listening Well . . . that's not precisely true.

Combine Although the author of the reading passage claims ....

.... ,

the professor states ....

....

2 **Reading** Since it takes in more oxygen, it grows taller and larger than many other wetland trees.

Listening The study determined that wetland cypress trees had no significantly higher levels of oxygen.

Combine Whereas the reading passage claims ....

.... ,

the professor claims that ....

....

3 **Reading** By growing more roots, plants in wetlands are better able to anchor themselves to the ground.

Listening However, these roots grow up and above the soil and are not actually in the ground beneath the water.

Combine The reading passage mentions that ....

.... ,

but the professor says that ....

....

4 **Reading** This keeps the tree from getting knocked over by high winds or flood conditions.

Listening There are horizontal roots beneath the soil that act as anchors though.

Combine While the reading passage states that ....

.... ,

the professor notes that ....

....

Review the notes from the reading and the listening. Complete the following chart with complete sentences.

Introduction	1 The lecture and the reading passage both discuss .... 2 However, the professor casts doubt on ....
Body 1	3 First, the professor covers .... 4 While the author of the reading passage declares that .... , the professor .... 5 She mentions a comparison between .... 6 According to her, ...
Body 2	7 Second, the professor does not agree with .... 8 She states that .... 9 Instead, horizontal roots ....
Conclusion (Optional)	10 As a result, the professor ....

Reading

The bald cypress is a tree that typically grows in swamps and other wetlands. It is noted for its distinct roots, which grow vertically out of the water and are sometimes called knees. These roots have two primary functions: to absorb oxygen and to anchor the tree to the ground.

Plants require oxygen in order to undergo photosynthesis to make food. Plants in wetlands such as swamps often have roots underwater, which makes it difficult to absorb oxygen from the air. Bald cypress roots, however, grow above the waterline. This allows the tree more easily to absorb oxygen from the air. Since it takes in more oxygen, it grows taller and larger than many other wetland trees.

The bald cypress also needs to anchor itself to the soil. Wetlands have loose soil because they are usually covered with water. By growing more roots, plants in wetlands are better able to anchor themselves to the ground. This keeps the tree from getting knocked over by high winds or flood conditions. The tree's roots also help absorb water from the wetlands, which makes the soil less loose. This, in turn, prevents soil erosion.

Listening

✎ Note Taking

01-07

Q Summarize the points made in the lecture, being sure to explain how they cast doubt on specific points made in the reading passage.

_____

_____

_____

_____

_____

_____

_____

_____

_____

_____

_____

_____

_____

_____

_____

_____

_____

Self-Evaluation Check your response by answering the following questions.

	Yes	No
1 Are all the important points from the lecture presented accurately?	☐	☐
2 Is the information from the lecture appropriately related to the reading?	☐	☐
3 Is the response well organized?	☐	☐
4 Are all the sentences grammatically correct?	☐	☐
5 Are all the words spelled correctly?	☐	☐
6 Are all the punctuation marks used correctly?	☐	☐

Exercise Read, listen, and answer the question following each step.

Reading Read the following passage and take notes.

Southern resident orcas, a distinct group of killer whales, are suffering a steady decline in their population. Marine biologists believe only seventy to eighty of them remain. The major issue for them concerns a lack of food.

Southern resident orcas live in the Pacific Ocean near the North American west coast. They depend on Chinook salmon as their primary food source. However, in recent years, the number of Chinook salmon in the Pacific has plummeted. The lack of food makes orcas weaker and more likely to become diseased due to pollutants. Pollutants such as PCBs are stored in orca blubber. When orcas cannot get salmon, they extract nutrients from their blubber. The PCBs are then released into their bodies, which can cause miscarriages in female orcas.

The orcas may also be stressed by noise from boats in their favored hunting areas. Orcas utilize echolocation, which is similar to radar, to find food. Orcas make noises, which are sent out and then bounce back to them from objects they hit. This action helps orcas find salmon to eat. However, noise from propellers can make echolocation not work properly. The orcas therefore have trouble finding food.

📖 Words & Phrases

distinct adj separate; noticeable
marine biologist n a scientist who focuses on sea creatures
concern v to be about
plummet v to go down greatly and quickly
pollutant n something that makes another thing dirty or unclean
blubber n fat stored in an animal's body

extract v to remove; to take out
miscarriage n the spontaneous death of a fetus inside a female's body
echolocation n the process of detecting objects by emitting sound waves that bounce back to the creature or thing emitting them
propeller n a device with rotating blades that helps a boat or ship move in the water

---

✏ Note Taking

Southern Resident Orcas – 2 Reason for Decline

1 Decreasing number of [1) _____]

- Primary food source ➔ hard to find now
- Pollutants in [2) _____] ➔ make whales have miscarriages

2 [3) _____] by noise from boats

- Use [4) _____] to catch fish
- Propeller noise makes echolocation not work ➔ have trouble finding food

Listening   Listen to a lecture on the topic you just read about and take notes.

✎ Note Taking

Southern Resident Orca Decline – Problems with Theories

01 - 08

1   Claim orcas cannot find enough food

- Other $^{1)}$ _____ in same areas ➔ can find enough food
- Other orcas and whales absorb pollutants ➔ no problem producing $^{2)}$ _____

2   Other animals $^{3)}$ _____ by noise

- Noise level measured ➔ similar to noise from $^{4)}$ _____
- No evidence storm noise prevents orcas from finding food

📖 Words & Phrases

steadily adv constantly

theory n a belief proposed to explain something

expert n a person with a special skill or knowledge

traditional adj following established behavior or actions

hunting ground n a place where a human or animal often hunts for food

reside v to live

offspring n the product of the reproductive action of a person or animal; an immediate descendent

fail v unsuccessfully to do something; not to do something well or properly

measure v to determine the amount, size, quantity, etc. of something

evidence n proof

Comparing the Points   Complete the main points from both notes as complete sentences.

Reasons for Orca Decline

Reading (Main Points)	**Listening** (Main Points)
Southern resident orcas' main food source, Chinook salmon, are disappearing, so the whales cannot _____. They have pollutants in their blubber, and when it gets released into their bodies, it causes _____.	Other orcas and whales live in the same _____, but they can find food with no problems. They also _____ the same pollutants but can produce offspring.
_____ disturbs the echolocation that orcas use to hunt. As a result, the orcas have _____ finding food.	Other orcas and whales are not affected by the _____ noise. It is as loud as a _____ in the ocean, and orcas can usually find food during storms.

Paraphrasing & Summarizing

A The following pairs of sentences are based on the reading. Complete each paraphrase by filling in the blanks with appropriate words or phrases. Then, complete the following summary.

1 Southern resident orcas, a distinct group of killer whales, are suffering a steady decline in their population.

→ A group of killer whales _____ southern resident orcas are seeing their numbers _____.

2 However, in recent years, the number of Chinook salmon in the Pacific has plummeted.

→ Lately, the Chinook salmon _____ is

_____.

3 The PCBs are then released into their bodies, which can cause miscarriages in female orcas.

→ The PCBs _____ their bodies and then make females

_____.

4 Orcas make noises, which are sent out and then bounce back to them from objects they hit.

→ Orcas _____ that reflect back to them from

_____.

5 However, noise from propellers can make echolocation not work properly.

→ But _____ makes orcas' radar _____.

📝 Summary

Southern resident orcas are dealing with a declining population. They mostly eat Chinook salmon, but the number of salmon is _____. The orcas cannot get _____. They also get pollutants like _____ in their blubber. When PCBs get into their bodies, _____ can have miscarriages. Orcas are also stressed by noise from _____. These cause their echolocation not to work properly, so they have trouble finding food.

B The following pairs of sentences are based on the listening. Complete each paraphrase by filling in the blanks with appropriate words or phrases. Then, complete the following summary.

1 In the past few decades, the southern resident orca population has been steadily declining.

→ _____, the number of southern resident orcas has been

_____ .

2 For example, some experts claim orcas cannot find enough food in their traditional hunting grounds.

→ _____, some state that orcas cannot catch enough food where

_____ .

3 They also absorb the same pollutants yet have no problem producing offspring.

→ They _____ the same pollutants but still

_____ .

4 Another theory states that noise from the propellers of boats is causing southern resident orcas to fail to find enough food.

→ Another thought is that propellers on boats are making _____

for orcas to _____ .

5 They have learned that the amount of noise is similar to that caused by storms in the ocean.

→ They know that _____ is the same as the noise made by

_____ .

✎ **Summary**

In recent decades, the southern resident orca population _____ . But there are some problems with the theories about why. _____ say orcas cannot find enough food in their hunting grounds. But other _____ can find food in the same places. They also have no problems _____ . Some also state that noise from boat propellers is disturbing orcas. But other orcas and whales _____ .

The following sentences are some important points from both the reading and the listening. Combine each pair of sentences to create your own sentence by using the given patterns.

1

Reading However, in recent years, the number of Chinook salmon in the Pacific has plummeted.

Listening You see, uh, other species of orcas and whales reside in the same areas. And they appear to have no problems finding food.

Combine Even though the author of the reading passage writes that ....
.... ,

the professor comments that ....
....

2

Reading The PCBs are then released into their bodies, which can cause miscarriages in female orcas.

Listening They also absorb the same pollutants yet have no problem producing offspring.

Combine While the reading passage notes that ....
.... ,

the professor remarks that ....
....

3

Reading The orcas may also be stressed by noise from boats in their favored hunting areas.

Listening Yet again, a comparison of other orcas and species of whales shows these animals are not affected.

Combine The reading passage claims that ....
.... ,

yet the professor states that ....
....

4

Reading However, noise from propellers can make echolocation not work properly.

Listening They have learned that the amount of noise is similar to that caused by storms in the ocean.

Combine Whereas the reading passage argues that ....
.... ,

the professor compares ....
....

Review the notes from the reading and the listening. Complete the following chart with complete sentences.

Introduction	1 The author of the reading passage discusses _____ _____.
	2 However, the professor challenges _____ _____.
Body 1	3 The reading passage notes that _____ _____.
	4 They are also _____ _____.
	5 However, the professor points out that _____ _____.
	6 He adds that _____ _____.
Body 2	7 Next, the reading passage covers _____ _____.
	8 While the author of the reading passage states that _____ _____, the professor remarks that _____.
	9 He mentions that _____ _____.
	10 Storms do not prevent _____ _____.
Conclusion (Optional)	11 The professor therefore shows _____ _____.

Reading

Southern resident orcas, a distinct group of killer whales, are suffering a steady decline in their population. Marine biologists believe only seventy to eighty of them remain. The major issue for them concerns a lack of food.

Southern resident orcas live in the Pacific Ocean near the North American west coast. They depend on Chinook salmon as their primary food source. However, in recent years, the number of Chinook salmon in the Pacific has plummeted. The lack of food makes orcas weaker and more likely to become diseased due to pollutants. Pollutants such as PCBs are stored in orca blubber. When orcas cannot get salmon, they extract nutrients from their blubber. The PCBs are then released into their bodies, which can cause miscarriages in female orcas.

The orcas may also be stressed by noise from boats in their favored hunting areas. Orcas utilize echolocation, which is similar to radar, to find food. Orcas make noises, which are sent out and then bounce back to them from objects they hit. This action helps orcas find salmon to eat. However, noise from propellers can make echolocation not work properly. The orcas therefore have trouble finding food.

Listening

✎ Note Taking

01-08

Q Summarize the points made in the lecture, being sure to explain how they challenge specific claims made in the reading passage.

_____

_____

_____

_____

_____

_____

_____

_____

_____

_____

_____

_____

_____

_____

_____

_____

Self-Evaluation Check your response by answering the following questions.

	Yes	No
1 Are all the important points from the lecture presented accurately?	☐	☐
2 Is the information from the lecture appropriately related to the reading?	☐	☐
3 Is the response well organized?	☐	☐
4 Are all the sentences grammatically correct?	☐	☐
5 Are all the words spelled correctly?	☐	☐
6 Are all the punctuation marks used correctly?	☐	☐

Exercise Read, listen, and answer the question following each step.

Reading Read the following passage and take notes.

Many people have a habit of purchasing large amounts of clothing which they rarely wear over time. These used clothes take up space, so people often suggest recycling these clothes. They can be dropped off in donation boxes or at sites that handle used clothing. However, recycling used clothes is not actually a wise option.

For one, there are many expenses required to recycle used clothing. Clothing donation boxes are typically made of sheet steel or high-quality plastic. This makes them expensive to build. They must also be serviced daily, so someone must be paid to empty their contents. In addition, the clothing must then be transported on trucks to recycling centers. The trucks, the fuel, and the drivers' salaries cost even more money.

A second issue concerns the pollution created by recycling used clothing. The trucks that carry clothes to recycling plants burn fuel. This expels pollutants into the air. The recycling plant itself utilizes fuel and electricity, which thereby creates more pollution. Finally, much of the clothing donated is unsuitable for recycling. As a result, it ends up in landfills, creating even more pollution.

📖 **Words & Phrases**

drop off v to take something to a place and to leave it there
donation n a gift given to someone
wise adj showing good judgment or reason
option n a choice
service v to provide maintenance for something

content n something that is found inside another thing
salary n the money a person earns for working
expel v to cast out; to throw out
unsuitable adj not appropriate; not right
landfill n a garbage dump; a place where garbage is taken

🖉 Note Taking

Problems with Recycling Used Clothing

1   Many expenses required to recycle clothes
   • 1)_____ boxes + service personnel → high expenses
   • Transporting clothes on trucks → expensive
   • Must pay for 2)_____, and drivers' salaries

2   Recycling clothes creates pollution
   • Trucks and 3)_____ burn fuel + expel pollutants
   • Much clothing 4)_____ → sent to landfills = creates pollution

Listen to a lecture on the topic you just read about and take notes.

✎ Note Taking

Recycling Used Clothes – Not Too Many Problems

01-09

1 Donate to [1)] _____

- Sell for low prices
- Money earned → donate to charity or social projects
- Creates [2)] _____ + improves people's lives

2 Making new clothes to replace old ones = more pollution

- Need [3)] _____ + water to grow cotton
- Transportation to [4)] _____ and stores → more pollution

📖 Words & Phrases

ton (n) 1,000 kilograms

generate (v) to create; to make

serious (adj) major; important

retailer (n) a store that sells small quantities of items

mend (v) to fix; to repair

earn (v) to make money

charity (n) an organization that helps others

cotton (n) a plant whose fibers are used to make cloth

pesticide (n) poison used to kill pests

textile mill (n) a place that produces cloth and fabric

Comparing the Points   Complete the main points from both notes as complete sentences.

Recycling Used Clothing

Reading (Main Points)	Listening (Main Points)
There are _____ such as clothing donation boxes and paying people who serve them when it comes to recycling used clothing. Transporting them to _____ costs even more money.	People can donate used clothing to retailers, who sell it for _____. The money is donated to charity or used for _____, so wealth is created, and people's lives are improved.
Recycling used clothing also creates pollution, such as by trucks and _____. In addition, donated clothing is sometimes unsuitable, so it goes to _____, which makes more pollution.	Making new clothes creates _____ than recycling used clothes. Growing cotton, _____ it to textile mills, and then sending clothes to stores all create lots of pollution.

Paraphrasing & Summarizing

A The following pairs of sentences are based on the reading. Complete each paraphrase by filling in the blanks with appropriate words or phrases. Then, complete the following summary.

1 Many people have a habit of purchasing large amounts of clothing which they rarely wear over time.

→ Many people buy _____ but _____ wear it.

2 Clothing donation boxes are typically made of sheet steel or high-quality plastic.

→ Boxes used clothes _____ are built with

_____ .

3 The trucks, the fuel, and the drivers' salaries cost even more money.

→ It _____ for trucks, fuel, and drivers'

_____ .

4 The recycling plant itself utilizes fuel and electricity, which thereby creates more pollution.

→ The _____ makes more pollution from the fuel and electricity

_____ .

5 Finally, much of the clothing donated is unsuitable for recycling.

→ A lot of _____ cannot _____ .

✎ Summary

Lots of people donate their _____ , but that is not always a smart thing to do. Among the expenses of donating clothing are the donation boxes and the _____ of those servicing them. Transporting the clothes to _____ requires additional payments. Recycling used clothes _____ , too. The trucks and the recycling plants use fuel that makes pollution. And many clothes cannot be recycled, so they go to _____ , which makes even more pollution.

B The following pairs of sentences are based on the listening. Complete each paraphrase by filling in the blanks with appropriate words or phrases. Then, complete the following summary.

1 In the United States alone, around eleven million tons of used clothes are generated each year.

→ .... produce around eleven million tons of used clothes ....

2 Rather than sending undesired clothing to recycling plants, people can take it to used clothing retailers.

→ .... recycling used clothes, people can give them to ....

3 The money earned from these sales is often donated to charity or used to fund various social projects.

→ .... from sales may be given to charity or used to .... social projects.

4 Yet making new clothes to replace old ones creates even more pollution.

→ But more pollution .... when people ....

5 Once the clothes are made, they are transported to stores, which creates even more pollution.

→ .... , they .... to stores, which makes more pollution.

✎ Summary

It is not right to say that recycling used clothes is expensive and .... First, people can donate used clothes to stores that sell them. Then, the money is often .... to charity or used for social projects. So recycling used clothes can .... and help others. Next, making new clothes produces .... than recycling old clothes. The costs include growing cotton and .... and then taking clothes to stores.

The following sentences are some important points from both the reading and the listening. Combine each pair of sentences to create your own sentence by using the given patterns.

1   **Reading**   Clothing donation boxes are typically made of sheet steel or high-quality plastic. This makes them expensive to build.

   Listening   Rather than sending undesired clothing to recycling plants, people can take it to used clothing retailers.

   Combine   The author of the reading passage describes ....

   ....,

   so the professor suggests that ....

   ....

2   **Reading**   The trucks, the fuel, and the drivers' salaries cost even more money.

   Listening   The money earned from these sales is often donated to charity or used to fund various social projects.

   Combine   While the reading passage mentions ....

   ....,

   the professor says that ....

   ....

3   **Reading**   The recycling plant itself utilizes fuel and electricity, which thereby creates more pollution.

   Listening   Farmers need pesticides and water to grow cotton.

   Combine   Although the reading passage states that ....

   ....,

   the professor points out ....

   ....

4   **Reading**   As a result, it ends up in landfills, creating even more pollution.

   Listening   Once the clothes are made, they are transported to stores, which creates even more pollution.

   Combine   Whereas the reading passage states that ....

   ....,

   the professor remarks that ....

   ....

Review the notes from the reading and the listening. Complete the following chart with complete sentences.

Introduction	1 Both the lecture and the reading passage focus on .... 2 In her talk, the professor challenges ....
Body 1	3 While the reading passage describes .... , the professor says that .... 4 Then, these stores will .... 5 The money is often donated ....
Body 2	6 Next, the professor refutes .... 7 The author claims that .... 8 But the professor counters that argument by stating that .... 9 For instance, ...
Conclusion (Optional)	10 By focusing on these two arguments, the professor challenges ....

Reading

Many people have a habit of purchasing large amounts of clothing which they rarely wear over time. These used clothes take up space, so people often suggest recycling these clothes. They can be dropped off in donation boxes or at sites that handle used clothing. However, recycling used clothes is not actually a wise option.

For one, there are many expenses required to recycle used clothing. Clothing donation boxes are typically made of sheet steel or high-quality plastic. This makes them expensive to build. They must also be serviced daily, so someone must be paid to empty their contents. In addition, the clothing must then be transported on trucks to recycling centers. The trucks, the fuel, and the drivers' salaries cost even more money.

A second issue concerns the pollution created by recycling used clothing. The trucks that carry clothes to recycling plants burn fuel. This expels pollutants into the air. The recycling plant itself utilizes fuel and electricity, which thereby creates more pollution. Finally, much of the clothing donated is unsuitable for recycling. As a result, it ends up in landfills, creating even more pollution.

Listening

> ✎ Note Taking
>
> 01-09

Q Summarize the points made in the lecture, being sure to explain how they challenge specific arguments made in the reading passage.

Self-Evaluation Check your response by answering the following questions.

		Yes	No
1	Are all the important points from the lecture presented accurately?	☐	☐
2	Is the information from the lecture appropriately related to the reading?	☐	☐
3	Is the response well organized?	☐	☐
4	Are all the sentences grammatically correct?	☐	☐
5	Are all the words spelled correctly?	☐	☐
6	Are all the punctuation marks used correctly?	☐	☐

PART II

Writing for the Academic Discussion Task

In the academic discussion task, you will first be presented with a question by a professor that is written on a university online discussion board. You will then read two short responses by students in the class. These responses typically take opposite or different positions. Then, you must write your own response to the question posed by the professor. You will have 10 minutes to write an essay in response to the question. A typical essay is at least 100 words long.

Writing for an Academic Discussion Task

Overview

The second part of the Writing section of the TOEFL iBT is the TOEFL Writing for an Academic Discussion Task. This is a new task as of July 2023. You will see a question written by a university professor and then two responses by students. Your task is to write a response to the question. A typical response will be at least 100 words. You have ten minutes to write your response.

Question Types

1 Yes/No

Sometimes the professor asks a question and then requests that the students provide a yes-no answer. The professor may also ask the students if they agree or disagree with a statement. You should determine whether your answer to the question is yes or no or if you agree or disagree with the statement and then support your position with appropriate reasons and examples.

2 Preference

For these questions, the professor provides the students with a choice and asks them which of the two they prefer. You should determine which choice you prefer and then support your position with appropriate reasons and examples.

3 Open-Ended

The professor states a question that has no right or wrong answer but merely asks the students what they think about a topic. You should state your opinion regarding the question and then support your position with appropriate reasons and examples.

Useful Tips

1 The questions asked in this section come from a variety of topics. Many of the topics concern the environment and economics. But there are also questions based on sociology, political science, and other subjects in the liberal arts.

2 You do not require any specialized background knowledge to answer the professor's question. Simply read the question and the two students' responses, and then you can formulate your own answer.

3 Be sure to comment on the responses by both students.

4 Be sure to provide your own opinion. One way to do this is to add extra information to a comment made by one of the students.

5 The minimum response is 100 words, but you should try to write more than that.

6 There is no right or wrong answer. Simply defend your choice with good arguments and examples.

7 Try to write at least one complex sentence—a sentence with a conjunction such as *because*, *however*, *although*, or *since*—and two compound sentences—a sentence with a conjunction such as *and*, *but*, *or*, or *so* in your response. This will improve the quality of your writing and give you a chance to have a higher score.

Key Strategies

1 Brainstorming

- Read the professor's questions carefully to make sure that you understand it.
- Read each student's response to make sure that you understand their arguments.
- Brainstorm some ideas on scratch paper before you begin writing.

2 Outlining & Organizing

- Organize your response in outline form.
- Develop your ideas into complete sentences.
- Be sure to include an introductory statement as well as a conclusion.

3 Completing the Essay

- Make sure that your introductory statement is clear.
- Be sure to refer to the argument that each student makes.
- Provide clear reasons and examples.
- Write a concluding sentence.
- There is no need to write multiple paragraphs. Your entire response can be a single paragraph.

4 Writing & Checking Your Essay

- Read the professor's question and two student responses and plan your essay in 2 minutes.
- Spend 5-6 minutes writing your essay.
- Take 2-3 minutes to read over your essay to make changes and to find mistakes.
- Make sure you use proper grammar, have correct spelling, and write logical sentences.

Your professor is teaching a class on urban development. Write a post responding to the professor's question.

In your response you should:

- express and support your opinion
- make a contribution to the discussion

An effective response will contain at least 100 words. You will have 10 minutes to write it.

Professor Madison

I want to continue talking about life in urban centers. One problem that many city residents complain about is expensive housing costs. Buying a house or renting an apartment is too much money for them. What do you think cities should do to reduce the cost of housing? Why?

Kevin

Many cities lack sufficient housing. There are simply not enough houses and apartments for everyone. That is making the price of housing so expensive. The best solution is to construct more housing. Cities should build numerous apartment buildings because they can supply many housing units for urban residents.

Diana

I believe cities should improve public transportation to suburbs. That will make it easier for people to travel downtown and then back to their homes. As a result, more people will move out of cities to live in suburbs. This will help ease the housing crisis in big cities.

Sample Response

Introductory sentence While Kevin and Diana have good ideas, I believe cities should try something else. **Supporting Details 1** These days, many people work from their homes, so they do not go into offices anymore. This has resulted in there being empty office buildings throughout cities. **Topic sentence** Cities should acquire these empty buildings. Then, they should convert the offices into housing units. **Supporting Details 2** Doing that would create hundreds or even thousands of new homes. Since the city would own the buildings, it could determine the prices of owning or renting them. **Conclusion** By making the payments low, the city could help large numbers of people.

Exercise 1 Follow the directions in each step.

Brainstorming & Outlining

A Read the professor's comment and brainstorm some ideas. Then, use the outline to generate your ideas.

Professor
Jarvis

The environment is in poor condition these days. There are problems with ground, air, and water pollution. Many businesses, especially factories, are creators of pollution. Do you think businesses should do more to protect the environment? Or do they not have a responsibility to do anything? Why or why not?

📖 Words & Phrases

poor adj bad
condition n a state of being
pollution n the state of being dirty or unclean

factory n a building where goods are manufactured
protect v to keep safe

❯ Outline for Brainstorming

Businesses Should Do More to Protect the Environment			
Agree		**Disagree**	
Reason 1	**Reason 2**	**Reason 1**	**Reason 2**
Are ones polluting it	Should clean up their messes	Are following government regulations	If obey law, don't need to clean up

B Read the following comments by two students and complete the summary notes.

Russell

Businesses definitely must do more to protect the environment. After all, they are the ones polluting it. They are the ones causing problems around the world. They need to provide funds to clean up the messes they create. And they need to stop creating so much pollution.

📖 **Words & Phrases**

definitely adj for sure; surely
pollute v to make dirty or unclean
provide v to make available

funds n money that can be spent
mess n a disordered or problematic situation

✏️ **Summary Notes: Russell**

Agree

1 Are ones 1) _____
  • Must do 2) _____
  • Are causing problems 3) _____

2 Need to provide 4) _____
  • Clean up 5) _____ they create
  • Stop 6) _____ so much pollution

Martina

I do not believe businesses need to do anything about the pollution they create. After all, the government has regulations they must follow. The government clearly believes creating some pollution is acceptable. Since businesses are obeying the law, they do not need to do anything else.

📖 **Words & Phrases**

government n the group of people responsible for running a country
regulation n a rule; a law

acceptable adj good enough
obey v to follow
law n a complete body of rules people must follow

✏️ **Summary Notes: Martina**

Disagree

1 No need to 1) _____
  • Government has 2) _____
  • Businesses 3) _____ them
  • Government believes 4) _____ = acceptable

2 Businesses 5) _____
  • No 6) _____ to do anything else

Organization Review the outline and the summary notes on the previous pages and then complete each chart.

▶ Supporting Russell's Opinion

Introduction	**1** While I understand _____ , I believe _____ .
Body 1	**2** As Russell points out, _____ . **3** In my city, _____ . **4** It should _____ .
Body 2	**5** In addition, _____ . **6** They _____ . **7** If they _____ , the world _____ .
Conclusion	**8** Businesses therefore must _____ .

▶ Supporting Martina's Opinion

Introduction	**1** I agree with Martina and _____ .
Body 1	**2** Martina is correct that _____ . **3** The government _____ . **4** But that _____ .
Body 2	**5** Another point is that _____ . **6** So many people _____ . **7** They _____ . **8** Individuals _____ .
Conclusion	**9** We should not _____ .

Exercise 2 Follow the directions and write a response. You can refer to the outline and the summary notes.

Q Your professor is teaching a class on environmental science. Write a post responding to the professor's question.

In your response you should:

- express and support your opinion
- make a contribution to the discussion

An effective response will contain at least 100 words. You will have 10 minutes to write it.

Professor Merriweather

In Thursday's class, we will discuss the recycling process. In recent decades, recycling has become common. Many governments both require and encourage it. Not everybody supports it though. Do you believe people should recycle more? Or is recycling not really beneficial to the environment? Why?

📖 **Words & Phrases**

recycling n the act of saving materials to use them again
process n a course of action
require v to command; to make something necessary to do

encourage v to try to persuade
beneficial adj helpful

❯ **Outline for Brainstorming**

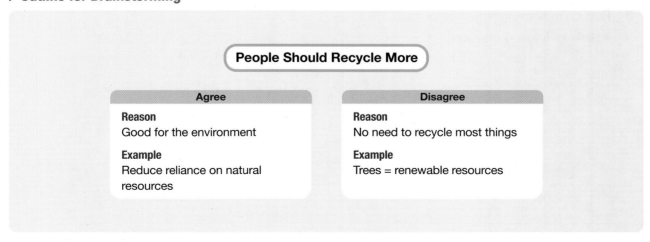

People Should Recycle More

Agree	Disagree
Reason Good for the environment	**Reason** No need to recycle most things
Example Reduce reliance on natural resources	**Example** Trees = renewable resources

Emily

Recycling is so good for the environment. People absolutely must recycle more. Thanks to improvements in technology, we can recycle all kinds of items. This reduces our reliance on natural resources and saves them for future generations.

Robert

There is no need to recycle most things. For instance, trees are renewable resources, so we do not need to recycle paper. Glass comes from silicon. That is available in abundant quantities all over the Earth. We just do not need to recycle as much as we do today.

 Words & Phrases

absolutely adv totally; for sure
improvement n the act of making something better
technology n the practical application of knowledge
reliance n the act of depending on someone or something
natural resource n a material that is found in nature

renewable resource n a material that is found in nature and that can be constantly supplied
glass n a transparent material made from silicates
silicon n an element that has many practical uses and is found in sand
abundant adj existing in large amounts; plentiful
quantity n an amount

Summary Notes

Emily
1 Recycling = good for environment
• Must recycle more
2 Improved technology = recycle all kinds of items
3 Reduce reliance on natural resources
• Save for future generations

Robert
1 No need to recycle most things
• Trees = renewable resources ➡ don't recycle paper
• Glass from silicon ➡ abundant on Earth
2 No need to recycle as much as do today

_____

_____

_____

_____

_____

_____

_____

_____

_____

_____

_____

_____

_____

Self-Evaluation   Check your response by answering the following questions.

	Yes	No
1 Did you address the professor's question?	☐	☐
2 Did you refer to the comments by the two students?	☐	☐
3 Did you express your own opinion?	☐	☐
4 Did you provide examples to support your opinion?	☐	☐
5 Did you organize your response well?	☐	☐
6 Did you use correct grammar?	☐	☐
7 Did you use correct punctuation?	☐	☐
8 Did you spell all of the words correctly?	☐	☐

Unit 10 Education I

Exercise 1 Follow the directions in each step.

Brainstorming & Outlining

A Read the professor's comment and brainstorm some ideas. Then, use the outline to generate your ideas.

Professor
Cartwright

Let's talk about high school curriculums. Most schools focus on academic subjects, such as math, science, and history. However, some also teach basic life skills, including cooking, cleaning, and managing personal finances. Do you think all high schools should teach basic life skills or only teach academic subjects? Why?

📖 **Words & Phrases**

curriculum n the courses offered at a school
academic adj relating to school
life skill n an ability that lets a person live life well

manage v to handle; to take care of
finance n the management of money

❯ **Outline for Brainstorming**

Basic Life Skills vs. Academic Subjects at High School			
Basic Life Skills		**Academic Subjects**	
Reason 1 Students have no practical knowledge	**Reason 2** Should have home economics classes	**Reason 1** Students need academic knowledge	**Reason 2** Parents can teach basic life skills

B Read the following comments by two students and complete the summary notes.

Sandra

I wish high schools would teach basic life skills. So many students graduate with book knowledge but no practical knowledge. High schools need to start teaching home economics classes to help students with life after graduation.

📖 **Words & Phrases**

wish v to want; to desire
graduate v to complete a course of study at a school
knowledge n the fact of knowing something

practical n useful
home economics n a class that teaches skills useful in a home

✏️ **Summary Notes:** Sandra

Basic Life Skills

1 High schools should teach 1) ....
  • Students have 2) ....
  • No 3) ....

2 Teach students 4) ....
  • Help w/life 6) ....

Wilson

The objective of schools should be teaching academic subjects. Students need to obtain knowledge of math, science, history, and other similar topics in high school. As for basic life skills, those are the responsibility of the students' parents. Schools should not be concerned about them.

📖 **Words & Phrases**

objective n a goal
obtain v to get; to acquire
topic n a subject

responsibility n accountability
concerned adj worried about; interested in

✏️ **Summary Notes:** Wilson

Academic Subjects

1 School objective = teaching 1) ....
  • Students should learn 2) ...., history, etc.

2 Basic life skills = 3) .... of students' parents
  • Schools should not be 4) .... w/them

Review the outline and the summary notes on the previous pages and then complete each chart.

▶ **Supporting Sandra's Opinion**

Introduction	1 Sandra is correct in stating that _____ .
Body 1	2 My older sister _____ .
	3 She _____ .
	4 It took her _____ .
Body 2	5 In addition, _____ .
	6 Academics are important but _____ .
	7 That is why _____ .
Conclusion	8 Adding classes in basic life skills _____ .

▶ **Supporting Wilson's Opinion**

Introduction	1 I like _____ .
Body 1	2 High school students _____ .
	3 Teaching basic life skills is _____ .
	4 My parents _____ .
	5 I know _____ .
Body 2	6 In addition, _____ .
	7 Colleges do not care _____ .
	8 They only care about _____ .
	9 High schools should therefore _____ .
Conclusion	10 The only topics _____ .

Exercise 2 Follow the directions and write a response. You can refer to the outline and the summary notes.

Q Your professor is teaching a class on education. Write a post responding to the professor's question.

In your response you should:

- express and support your opinion
- make a contribution to the discussion

An effective response will contain at least 100 words. You will have 10 minutes to write it.

Professor
Holmes

The price of college tuition is incredibly high nowadays. Many students cannot afford to pay tuition, so they take out loans. Unfortunately, many students have huge amounts of debt now. Here is an idea: The government should eliminate all student loans. Do you agree or disagree? Why or why not?

📖 **Words & Phrases**

tuition (n) the price of payment for a class, school, etc.
incredibly (adv) very; highly
afford (v) to have enough money to pay for something

loan (n) money lent to a person, who must pay interest on it
eliminate (v) to get rid of; to wipe out

❯ **Outline for Brainstorming**

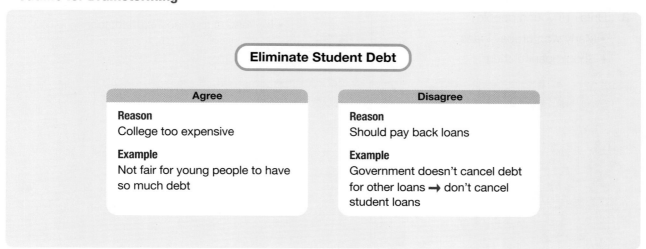

Eliminate Student Debt

Agree	Disagree
Reason College too expensive	**Reason** Should pay back loans
Example Not fair for young people to have so much debt	**Example** Government doesn't cancel debt for other loans → don't cancel student loans

Ernest

I agree that the government should cancel all student loans. Attending college is absurdly expensive. However, people need to attend college to get jobs. It is unfair for young people to have so much debt. Many will never repay their loans, so the loans should be canceled.

Sally

I strongly disagree with the statement. The students who took out the loans should pay them back. That is the proper thing to do. The government does not cancel debt for people with vehicle loans or mortgages. There is therefore no reason to do that for student loans.

📖 Words & Phrases

cancel (v) to destroy; to get rid of
absurdly (adv) ridiculously; terribly
unfair (adj) not just or right
debt (n) money a person owes
repay (v) to pay back money a person owes
strongly (adv) powerfully; greatly

pay back (v) to pay a person money that was lent
proper (adj) correct; right
vehicle (n) a means of transporting things, such as a car, bus, and train
mortgage (n) a loan for a house or property

✏️ Summary Notes

Ernest	Sally

1   Should cancel student loans
    • Attending college = too expensive
 	
2   Must attend college to get a job
 	
3   Unfair to young people
    • Many won't repay loans
    • Should cancel them
	1 Should pay back loans took out
	    • Is proper thing to do
	
	2 Government doesn't cancel vehicle loans or mortgages
	    • No reason to cancel student loans

_____

_____

_____

_____

_____

_____

_____

_____

_____

_____

_____

_____

_____

_____

_____

_____

Self-Evaluation Check your response by answering the following questions.

	Yes	No
1 Did you address the professor's question?	☐	☐
2 Did you refer to the comments by the two students?	☐	☐
3 Did you express your own opinion?	☐	☐
4 Did you provide examples to support your opinion?	☐	☐
5 Did you organize your response well?	☐	☐
6 Did you use correct grammar?	☐	☐
7 Did you use correct punctuation?	☐	☐
8 Did you spell all of the words correctly?	☐	☐

Exercise 1 Follow the directions in each step.

Brainstorming & Outlining

A Read the professor's comment and brainstorm some ideas. Then, use the outline to generate your ideas.

Professor Lamplighter

I would like you to think about free-time and leisure activities now. When people have free time, they engage in a number of different activities. Do you prefer to do free-time activities alone? Or do you prefer to do them together with other people? Why?

📖 Words & Phrases

free-time n a time when a person can do anything he or she wants
leisure n time free from work, school, or other duties

engage v to take part in; to do
alone adv by oneself
together adv with another person; with others

❯ Outline for Brainstorming

Do Free-Time Activities Alone or with Others

Alone		With Others	
Reason 1	**Reason 2**	**Reason 1**	**Reason 2**
Enjoy painting pictures	Make model airplanes and ships	Love hiking w/brother	Watch movies w/friends

B Read the following comments by two students and complete the summary notes.

Calvin

My hobbies are all activities I do by myself, so I prefer being alone. I enjoy painting landscapes and still lifes in my free time. In addition, I sometimes make models of airplanes and ships. They are not the types of activities you can do with another person.

📕 **Words & Phrases**

painting (n) the act of putting paint on canvas or another place

landscape (n) a picture of nature

still life (n) a picture of inanimate objects

model (n) a small representation of something

type (n) a kind

✏️ **Summary Notes:** Calvin

Alone
1 Enjoy 1) _____
• Paint 2) _____ and 3) _____
2 Make 4) _____
• Make models of 5) _____ and 6) _____

Shannon

When I do leisure activities, I am always with someone. For instance, I love going hiking at a local national park. This is an activity I frequently do with my brother. Another free-time activity of mine is watching movies. My close friends and I often see a movie every weekend.

📕 **Words & Phrases**

local (adj) nearby

national park (n) an area of importance made into a park by the government

frequently (adv) often

weekend (n) Saturday and Sunday

✏️ **Summary Notes:** Shannon

With Others
1 Enjoy 1) _____ at national park
• Do w/ 2) _____
2 Watch 3) _____
• See w/ 4) _____ on 5) _____

Organization Review the outline and the summary notes on the previous pages and then complete each chart.

▶ Supporting Calvin's Opinion

Introduction	1 Calvin and I _____ because _____.
Body 1	2 While he enjoys _____, I prefer _____. 3 I _____ 4 For me, _____.
Body 2	5 Another hobby _____. 6 We have _____, and I _____. 7 I mostly play pop songs, but I also _____.
Conclusion	8 These two hobbies are _____.

▶ Supporting Shannon's Opinion

Introduction	1 While I understand _____, my style is _____.
Body 1	2 However, I _____. 3 One of my hobbies is _____. 4 My best friend and I _____. 5 We _____.
Body 2	6 Another _____. 7 My mother and I _____. 8 It is _____, and I love _____.
Conclusion	9 These hobbies _____.

Exercise 2 Follow the directions and write a response. You can refer to the outline and the summary notes.

Q Your professor is teaching a class on sociology. Write a post responding to the professor's question.

In your response you should:

- express and support your opinion
- make a contribution to the discussion

An effective response will contain at least 100 words. You will have 10 minutes to write it.

Professor
Benjamin

Nowadays, social media is extremely popular with many people, especially the young. There are many influencers on social media. These individuals have thousands or millions of followers who listen carefully to what they say. Do you believe social media influencers have a positive or negative effect on people? Why?

📖 **Words & Phrases**

extremely adv very
influencer n a person who has an effect on others
individual n a person

positive adj beneficial; good
negative adj harmful; bad

❯ **Outline for Brainstorming**

Social Media Influencers: Positive or Negative

Positive	Negative
Reason Good messages on podcasts	**Reason** Terrible people
Example Encourage followers to listen to parents	**Example** Engage in immoral behavior

Ronald

Overall, I would say most social media influencers have a positive effect on their followers. I watch some influencers' podcasts. They tell their followers to eat nutritious food, to pay attention to their parents, and to be good. In my mind, their advice has a positive effect on others.

Christina

Most social media influencers are terrible people to whom nobody should listen. So many influencers become popular for bad reasons. These people often engage in immoral behavior, and they negatively affect the lives of many people, especially teens.

📖 Words & Phrases

overall adv generally; as a whole

podcast n a program a person can watch on the Internet

nutritious adj healthy; good for the body

pay attention phr to listen closely

advice n a recommendation on how to act

terrible adj very bad; awful

immoral adj not moral; going against accepted traditions and behaviors

affect v to act on and to cause something to happen

especially adv particularly

📝 Summary Notes

Ronald
1 Most have positive effect
2 Influencers have podcasts
• Tell followers to eat nutritious food
• Pay attention to parents
• Be good
3 Advice has positive effect

Christina
1 Social influencers = terrible people
• People shouldn't listen to them
2 Become popular for bad reasons
• Engage in immoral behavior
• Negatively affect lives of many

_____

_____

_____

_____

_____

_____

_____

_____

_____

_____

_____

_____

_____

_____

_____

_____

📋 Self-Evaluation Check your response by answering the following questions.

	Yes	No
1 Did you address the professor's question?	☐	☐
2 Did you refer to the comments by the two students?	☐	☐
3 Did you express your own opinion?	☐	☐
4 Did you provide examples to support your opinion?	☐	☐
5 Did you organize your response well?	☐	☐
6 Did you use correct grammar?	☐	☐
7 Did you use correct punctuation?	☐	☐
8 Did you spell all of the words correctly?	☐	☐

Exercise 1 Follow the directions in each step.

Brainstorming & Outlining

A Read the professor's comment and brainstorm some ideas. Then, use the outline to generate your ideas.

Professor
Arbuckle

We are going to discuss after-school activities in our next class. Here is a topic for the discussion board. Many students participate in extracurricular activities after classes are dismissed. Would you prefer to play sports or to do club activities after school? Why?

📖 **Words & Phrases**

board n a bulletin board; a place to post information
participate v to do; to take part in
extracurricular adj relating to an organized student activity that is not a class

dismiss v to let out; to end
club n a group of people with a similar interest and who meet at times

❯ **Outline for Brainstorming**

Play Sports or Do Club Activities			

Play Sports		Do Club Activities	
Reason 1	**Reason 2**	**Reason 1**	**Reason 2**
Fun and great exercise	Like to belong to team	Can learn a lot	Fun to do

B Read the following comments by two students and complete the summary notes.

Ryan

I consider myself an athlete, so I would prefer to play sports after school. I enjoy team sports such as basketball and soccer. I like playing tennis as well. These activities are not only fun but are also great exercise. Furthermore, I love belonging to a team.

📖 **Words & Phrases**

consider v to believe; to think
athlete n a person who plays sports, often well
exercise n the act of moving one's body for the sake of getting fit

furthermore adv in addition; besides
belong v to be a part of

✏️ **Summary Notes: Ryan**

Play Sports

1 Consider self ¹⁾ _____
  • Play team sports ➜ ²⁾ _____ and ³⁾ _____
  • Also play tennis

2 Activities = fun + great exercise

3 Love belonging to ⁴⁾ _____

Candice

Given the two choices, I would select club activities. Many clubs are academic in nature. These include the math and science clubs. I can learn a lot by joining them. Other clubs, such as the chess and photography clubs, are for hobbies. Those would be fun to join, too.

📖 **Words & Phrases**

select v to choose
in nature phr having a certain quality or qualities
include v to contain

join v to become a part of
photography n the act of taking pictures

✏️ **Summary Notes: Candice**

Do Club Activities

1 ¹⁾ _____ clubs
  • Math and ²⁾ _____
  • Can ³⁾ _____ by joining

2 ⁴⁾ _____ clubs
  • For ⁵⁾ _____
  • Fun to ⁶⁾ _____

Organization   Review the outline and the summary notes on the previous pages and then complete each chart.

▶ **Supporting Ryan's Opinion**

Introduction	1 While ...., I would ....
Body 1	2 Ryan is correct .... 3 When I .... we always have a great time. 4 I also find that ....
Body 2	5 Another positive factor .... 6 It feels great to .... 7 There really is ....
Conclusion	8 For those reasons, ...

▶ **Supporting Candice's Opinion**

Introduction	1 I am like Candice and ....
Body 1	2 Clubs .... 3 I would like to .... 4 In those clubs, I could ....
Body 2	5 If I also ...., I could .... 6 That would .... while also ....
Conclusion	7 Those reasons are ....

Exercise 2 Follow the directions and write a response. You can refer to the outline and the summary notes.

Q Your professor is teaching a class on education. Write a post responding to the professor's question.

In your response you should:

- express and support your opinion
- make a contribution to the discussion

An effective response will contain at least 100 words. You will have 10 minutes to write it.

Professor Vernon

Scientific research has proved that children and teenagers do not get enough sleep at night. However, children and teens must typically wake up early to attend school. Do you think schools should start one hour later than normal to let students sleep more? Why or why not?

📖 **Words & Phrases**

research Ⓝ careful and in-depth study
prove Ⓥ to show to be true
teenager Ⓝ a person between the ages of thirteen and nineteen

typically adv usually
normal adj usual

❯ **Outline for Brainstorming**

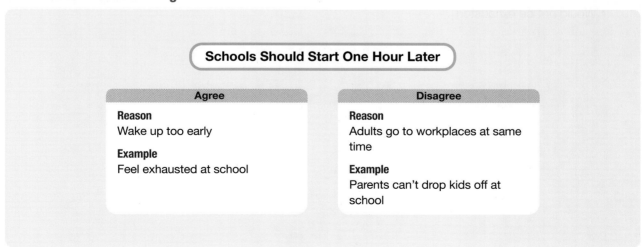

Schools Should Start One Hour Later

Agree	Disagree
Reason Wake up too early	**Reason** Adults go to workplaces at same time
Example Feel exhausted at school	**Example** Parents can't drop kids off at school

Andrew

I think it is a wonderful idea. I have to wake up around six every morning to attend school. That is simply too early since I normally go to bed at midnight. If school started later in the day, I would not always be so exhausted.

Melanie

It is an appealing idea, but I do not think schools should do that. Most adults go to their workplaces at the same time that students go to school. Parents would not be able to drop their children off at school if school started an hour later.

📖 **Words & Phrases**

wonderful adj great; very good
simply adv clearly
normally adv usually
midnight n twelve o'clock at night
exhausted adj very tired
appealing adj pleasing; satisfying

adult n a person eighteen years of age or older
workplace n the place where a person works
parent n the mother or father of a child
drop off v to take a person to a place and to let the person go

✏️ **Summary Notes**

Andrew

1 Wonderful idea
   • Wake up at 6:00 to attend school
   • Too early ➡ go to bed at midnight

2 If school started later
   • Would not be exhausted

Melanie

1 Adults go to workplaces
   • Same time students go to school

2 If school started later
   • Parents couldn't drop kids off at school

_____

_____

_____

_____

_____

_____

_____

_____

_____

_____

_____

_____

_____

_____

_____

Self-Evaluation Check your response by answering the following questions.

	Yes	No
1 Did you address the professor's question?	☐	☐
2 Did you refer to the comments by the two students?	☐	☐
3 Did you express your own opinion?	☐	☐
4 Did you provide examples to support your opinion?	☐	☐
5 Did you organize your response well?	☐	☐
6 Did you use correct grammar?	☐	☐
7 Did you use correct punctuation?	☐	☐
8 Did you spell all of the words correctly?	☐	☐

Exercise 1 Follow the directions in each step.

Brainstorming & Outlining

A Read the professor's comment and brainstorm some ideas. Then, use the outline to generate your ideas.

Professor
Redwood

We will talk about advertisements next Monday. Now, I want you to think about this. Most businesses advertise their goods and services. However, many ads are misleading. They make false claims or make their products look different than they really are. Should misleading advertisements be prohibited? Why or why not?

📖 Words & Phrases

advertisement n a paid notice; a notice promoting a company's product
good n something manufactured for sale

misleading adj pointing in the wrong direction, often on purpose
false adj fake; not true
claim n to say that something is true

❯ **Outline for Brainstorming**

Prohibit Misleading Advertisements

Agree		Disagree	
Reason 1	**Reason 2**	**Reason 1**	**Reason 2**
Made purchases because of ads	Didn't get products in pictures	Everyone knows ads bend the truth	Let the buyer beware

B Read the following comments by two students and complete the summary notes.

Kristine

I am strongly opposed to misleading advertisements. Companies should not be allowed to use them. I have occasionally made purchases because of ads. However, when I received the items, they did not resemble the pictures in the ads. That was wrong and should not be permitted.

📖 Words & Phrases

oppose Ⓥ to be against someone or something
occasionally adv sometimes
purchase ⓝ the act of buying something

resemble Ⓥ to look like; to be similar to
permit Ⓥ to allow

✏️ Summary Notes: Kristine

Agree
1 Strongly opposed to 1)_____
• 2)_____ shouldn't be allowed to use them
2 Have made purchases due to 3)_____
• Received items → didn't 4)_____ in ads
• Wrong → should not be 5)_____

Edward

There is nothing wrong with misleading advertisements. Consumers should always be wary of ads. Everyone knows that ads bend the truth and never bring up anything negative about products. Yet people still get fooled by them. That is their problem, not the company's problem.

📖 Words & Phrases

consumer ⓝ a shopper; a buyer
wary adj cautious; suspicious; careful about
bend the truth phr to say something that is not true or is misleading

bring up Ⓥ to state; to mention
get fooled phr to be tricked

✏️ Summary Notes: Edward

Disagree
1 1)_____ w/misleading ads
• 2)_____ = be wary of ads
2 Ads 3)_____
• Never bring up 4)_____ info about products
• People 5)_____ by them

Organization
Review the outline and the summary notes on the previous pages and then complete each chart.

▶ Supporting Kristine's Opinion

Introduction	1 I understand _____, but I _____.
Body 1	2 Kristine is correct in stating _____.
	3 I too _____.
	4 As a result, _____.
	5 I do not _____.
Body 2	6 In addition, children _____.
	7 They _____.
	8 It simply is not fair _____.
Conclusion	9 Misleading ads _____.

▶ Supporting Edward's Opinion

Introduction	1 While _____, these ads _____.
Body 1	2 First, we should _____.
	3 This means _____.
	4 They should not _____.
Body 2	5 Second, people _____.
	6 Even lying _____.
	7 So _____.
	8 When _____, they will _____.
	9 Then, it will _____.
Conclusion	10 That is _____.

Exercise 2 Follow the directions and write a response. You can refer to the outline and the summary notes.

Q Your professor is teaching a class on economics. Write a post responding to the professor's question.

In your response you should:

- express and support your opinion
- make a contribution to the discussion

An effective response will contain at least 100 words. You will have 10 minutes to write it.

Professor
Nash

Small businesses are important to the country's economy. Small businesses often have two or more owners. In many instances, the owners are friends. Friends can work well together yet can also encounter serious problems. Do you believe people should go into business with friends? Why or why not?

📖 **Words & Phrases**

economy ⓝ all of the economic activity in a region
instance ⓝ a situation; an example

encounter ⓥ to meet; to experience
serious ⓐⓓⓙ important; severe

❯ **Outline for Brainstorming**

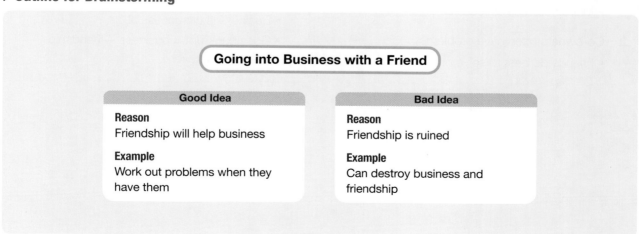

Going into Business with a Friend

Good Idea	Bad Idea
Reason Friendship will help business	**Reason** Friendship is ruined
Example Work out problems when they have them	**Example** Can destroy business and friendship

Isabella

I believe friends should go into business together. Because of their friendship, they will work diligently to make their business successful. Many co-owners have problems with each other. But friends in business together will do their best to work out their problems.

Bernard

It is an awful idea for friends to go into business together. So many friendships are ruined when a business is unsuccessful and goes bankrupt. When that happens, both the business and the friendship are destroyed forever.

📖 Words & Phrases

go into business phr to start a business
friendship n the act of being friends with someone
diligently adv hard; energetically
co-owner n one of two owners of a business
do one's best phr to try as hard as one can
solve v to find an answer to a problem
ruin v to end; to damage something so that it cannot be fixed

unsuccessful adj not successful; not having a positive outcome
go bankrupt phr to lose all of one's money; to go out of business
destroy v to kill; to ruin; to end
forever adv for all time

✏️ Summary Notes

Isabella
1 Should go into business together
• Friendship = work diligently
• Make business successful
2 Co-owners often have problems
• Friends do best to solve problems

Bernard
1 Awful idea
2 Friendships are ruined
• Business is unsuccessful
• Goes bankrupt = business + friendship destroyed forever

（ruled writing lines — blank）

Self-Evaluation Check your response by answering the following questions.

	Yes	No
1 Did you address the professor's question?	☐	☐
2 Did you refer to the comments by the two students?	☐	☐
3 Did you express your own opinion?	☐	☐
4 Did you provide examples to support your opinion?	☐	☐
5 Did you organize your response well?	☐	☐
6 Did you use correct grammar?	☐	☐
7 Did you use correct punctuation?	☐	☐
8 Did you spell all of the words correctly?	☐	☐

Unit 14　Sociology II

Exercise 1　Follow the directions in each step.

Brainstorming & Outlining

A　Read the professor's comment and brainstorm some ideas. Then, use the outline to generate your ideas.

Professor
Trent

People travel nowadays more often than in the past. It is common for people to take at least one trip a year. These trips may be domestic or foreign ones. When you travel, do you prefer to go somewhere in your own country, or would you rather visit a destination abroad? Why?

📖 Words & Phrases

common adj normal; usual
domestic adj of or relating to one's own country
foreign adj of or relating to a country other than one's own

somewhere adv in, at, or to an unspecified place
destination n the place where a person is going

❯ Outline for Brainstorming

Domestic or Foreign Trips

Domestic Trips		Foreign Trips	
Reason 1	**Reason 2**	**Reason 1**	**Reason 2**
Country has beautiful scenery	Can learn about homeland	Many exotic lands to visit	Visit sites of historical interest

B Read the following comments by two students and complete the summary notes.

Lionel

I have traveled abroad before, but I prefer to take domestic trips. My country is full of beautiful scenery, so there are numerous places to visit. I love learning about my homeland by visiting the natural wonders that can be seen here.

📖 **Words & Phrases**

travel abroad `phr` to travel to or in another country
scenery `n` a view, often pleasant to look at
homeland `n` the country that one is from

natural `adj` existing in nature; not made by humans
wonder `n` something that causes admiration or pleasure

✏️ **Summary Notes:** Lionel

Domestic Trips

1 Country = full of [1] ....
   • [2] .... places to visit

2 Learn about [3] ....
   • Visit [4] .... here

Sienna

I prefer traveling to other countries to taking a trip in my own nation. There are so many exotic lands to visit. I love to visit sites of historical interest as well as famous landmarks. Europe is the region I enjoy the most because of all the places to visit.

📖 **Words & Phrases**

exotic `adj` being from another country; mysterious; different
site `n` a place

historical `adj` relating to history
famous `adj` well known
landmark `n` a well-known building or structure

✏️ **Summary Notes:** Sienna

Foreign Trips

1 Many [1] .... to visit
   • Sites of [2] ....
   • Famous [3] ....

2 Enjoy going to [4] ....
   • Many [5] .... to visit

Organization Review the outline and the summary notes on the previous pages and then complete each chart.

▶ **Supporting Lionel's Opinion**

Introduction	1 Sienna _____, but I _____.
Body 1	2 Lionel is correct about _____ 3 I love _____ 4 I _____
Body 2	5 It is also important that _____ 6 My family _____ 7 We cannot _____
Conclusion	8 Those are _____

▶ **Supporting Sienna's Opinion**

Introduction	1 I like _____. 2 However, I _____.
Body 1	3 My family _____. 4 We saw _____. 5 It was _____.
Body 2	6 Additionally, _____. 7 I like to _____. 8 I also enjoy _____.
Conclusion	9 I can only _____.

Exercise 2 Follow the directions and write a response. You can refer to the outline and the summary notes.

Q Your professor is teaching a class on sociology. Write a post responding to the professor's question.

In your response you should:

- express and support your opinion
- make a contribution to the discussion

An effective response will contain at least 100 words. You will have 10 minutes to write it.

Professor
Cloniger

I want you to think about life following college now. Once students graduate, they often start their careers. Later, many get married and start a family. At times, people must choose between their career and their family. Which of these two is more important? Why?

📖 **Words & Phrases**

following adj coming afterward; next
once conj when; as soon as
career n a profession a person trains for and does as a permanent job

get married phr to wed; to make a person one's husband or wife
choose v to select; to make a choice

❯ **Outline for Brainstorming**

Career or Family

Career	Family
Reason High hopes for career	**Reason** Would pick family over everything
Example Expect to become executive → focus on career to achieve greatness	**Example** Cannot replace family; can always get new job

Matthew

My career is the more important of the two. I have high hopes for my career and expect to become an executive one day. I need to focus exclusively on it to achieve greatness. I cannot afford to let anything get in my way.

Stella

My family is more valuable than anything else. I would pick my family over everything. I can always obtain another job and start a new career in a different occupation. I cannot replace my family if something bad happens to them.

📖 Words & Phrases

hope n a desire; a wish for the future
expect v to believe something is certain to happen
executive n an administrator; a manager
exclusively adv only; solely
greatness n the quality of being very good
valuable adj worth a lot

pick v to choose; to select
obtain v to get; to acquire
occupation n a person's business; the work a person does
replace v to take the place of

✏️ Summary Notes

Matthew
1 Have high hopes for career
• Expect to become executive
2 Need to focus exclusively on career
• Can achieve greatness
• Letting nothing get in my way

Stella
1 Family = more valuable than anything else
2 Can always obtain another job
• Can start career in different occupation
• Cannot replace family

_____

_____

_____

_____

_____

_____

_____

_____

_____

_____

_____

_____

_____

Self-Evaluation Check your response by answering the following questions.

	Yes	No
1 Did you address the professor's question?	☐	☐
2 Did you refer to the comments by the two students?	☐	☐
3 Did you express your own opinion?	☐	☐
4 Did you provide examples to support your opinion?	☐	☐
5 Did you organize your response well?	☐	☐
6 Did you use correct grammar?	☐	☐
7 Did you use correct punctuation?	☐	☐
8 Did you spell all of the words correctly?	☐	☐

Exercise 1 Follow the directions in each step.

Brainstorming & Outlining

A Read the professor's comment and brainstorm some ideas. Then, use the outline to generate your ideas.

Professor Eco

Summer vacation for high school students tends to be at least two months long. During that time, many students acquire part-time jobs to earn money and to gain experience. Others do different activities, such as taking private lessons. Which activity do you believe high school students should do? Why?

📖 Words & Phrases

tend Ⓥ to have an inclination or tendency to do something
part-time adj doing some of the time
earn Ⓥ to make, as in money

experience Ⓝ practical skill, knowledge, or ability gained from doing an activity
lesson Ⓝ a class

❯ Outline for Brainstorming

Do Part-Time Job during Summer Vacation or Other Activities

Part-Time Jobs		Other Activities	
Reason 1 Earn spending money	**Reason 2** Gain experience	**Reason 1** Play musical instrument	**Reason 2** Take art lessons or learn foreign language

B Read the following comments by two students and complete the summary notes.

Jessica

Summer is the ideal time for high school students to work part time. They can earn spending money for the remainder of the year by doing various jobs. They can also gain experience that will teach them important skills. This will help them in the future.

📖 Words & Phrases

ideal adj best
spending money phr money a person has to use, not to save

remainder n the rest of something
gain v to earn
skill n an ability

✏️ Summary Notes: Jessica

Part-Time Jobs

1 Earn 1) _____
   • Use for 2) _____ of year
   • Do 3) _____

2 Gain 4) _____
   • Teach them 5) _____
   • Help them in 6) _____

Rudy

High school students should use the opportunity to do different activities. They could learn to play a musical instrument by taking private lessons. They could take art lessons or learn a foreign language, too. Because there is no school, they can focus on learning a new skill or ability.

📖 Words & Phrases

opportunity v a chance
musical instrument n a tool used to make music
foreign language n a language used in another country

focus v to concentrate on
ability n a skill

✏️ Summary Notes: Rudy

Other Activities

1 Learn to play 1) _____
   • Take 2) _____
   • Take 3) _____
   • Learn 4) _____

2 No school = focus on learning 5) _____

Review the outline and the summary notes on the previous pages and then complete each chart.

▶ Supporting Jessica's Opinion

Introduction	1 I like _____.
Body 1	2 High school students should _____.
	3 Then, they will _____.
	4 This will _____.
Body 2	5 Another reason is that _____.
	6 They can _____.
	7 They can also _____.
	8 They will _____.
Conclusion	9 That is why _____.

▶ Supporting Rudy's Opinion

Introduction	1 I agree with Rudy and think _____.
Body 1	2 Learning _____.
	3 My brother _____, and my sister _____.
	4 Those skills _____.
Body 2	5 In addition, _____.
	6 Students should _____.
	7 They should not _____.
	8 They can _____.
Conclusion	9 Instead, they ought to _____.

Exercise 2 Follow the directions and write a response. You can refer to the outline and the summary notes.

 Q Your professor is teaching a class on education. Write a post responding to the professor's question.

In your response you should:

- express and support your opinion
- make a contribution to the discussion

An effective response will contain at least 100 words. You will have 10 minutes to write it.

Professor
Peters

We will discuss volunteer work next Monday. Here is something to consider on the discussion board. Many schools require their students to volunteer at food kitchens, homeless shelters, or other places in their free time. Do you believe students should have to volunteer? Why or why not?

📖 **Words & Phrases**

volunteer Ⓥ to work for free, often to help others

require Ⓥ to make someone do something; to say that someone must do something

food kitchen Ⓝ a place that provides food to poor people

homeless shelter Ⓝ a place where people without homes can stay

free time Ⓝ time when a person can do whatever he or she wants

❯ **Outline for Brainstorming**

Should Students Volunteer

Agree	Disagree
Reason See how unfortunate people in society live	**Reason** Should not force students to volunteer
Example Volunteer where poor, unemployed, and homeless go	**Example** Students will be uninspired and have poor work ethic

Phillip

Schools should definitely make their students volunteer. Students need to see how unfortunate people in society live. They should therefore have to volunteer at places where poor, unemployed, and homeless people go. Volunteering at those places can teach students many lessons about life.

Fiona

It would be wrong for schools to force students to do volunteer work. After all, the word volunteer implies that people want to do something. If students are obligated to volunteer, most will be uninspired and have a poor work ethic. They will not benefit in any way.

📖 Words & Phrases

unfortunate adj unlucky
society n a broad group of people who live together
poor adj having little or no money
unemployed adj having no job
homeless adj having no home
force v to make a person do something

imply v to suggest without actually saying something
obligate v to make; to force
uninspired adj lacking desire or motivation
work ethic n the belief that one should work hard at one's job

✏️ Summary Notes

Phillip
1 Need to see how unfortunate people live
• Volunteer where poor, unemployed, and homeless go
2 Can teach students lessons about life

Fiona
1 Wrong to force students to volunteer
• Volunteer = implies want to do something
2 Obligate students to volunteer
• Will be uninspired + poor work ethic
• Will not benefit students

_____

_____

_____

_____

_____

_____

_____

_____

_____

_____

_____

_____

_____

_____

_____

_____

Self-Evaluation Check your response by answering the following questions.

		Yes	No
1	Did you address the professor's question?	☐	☐
2	Did you refer to the comments by the two students?	☐	☐
3	Did you express your own opinion?	☐	☐
4	Did you provide examples to support your opinion?	☐	☐
5	Did you organize your response well?	☐	☐
6	Did you use correct grammar?	☐	☐
7	Did you use correct punctuation?	☐	☐
8	Did you spell all of the words correctly?	☐	☐

Sociology III

Exercise 1 Follow the directions in each step.

Brainstorming & Outlining

A Read the professor's comment and brainstorm some ideas. Then, use the outline to generate your ideas.

Professor
Windsor

Next week, we will discuss population issues in our country. I want to know your thoughts on this. Many large urban centers are overpopulated. This is causing problems like traffic jams and high rents. What can cities do to relieve their population problems? Why do you think so?

📖 **Words & Phrases**

population n the number of people in a certain area
urban adj relating to a city
overpopulated adj having too many people in a certain area

traffic jam n a situation in which too many vehicles are on a road
relieve v to ease; to make better

❭ **Outline for Brainstorming**

How to Relieve Urban Population Problems

Move to Suburbs		Use Empty Land	
Reason 1	**Reason 2**	**Reason 1**	**Reason 2**
Encourage people to move to suburbs	Improve public transportation	Many abandoned buildings	Construct apartments or parks with them

B Read the following comments by two students and complete the summary notes.

Ashley

Cities should encourage people to live in suburbs. That way, people will be located near the cities where they work. However, they will not actually live in these cities. By improving public transportation such as subways and buses, cities can make the suburbs more appealing. Then, cities' populations will decline.

📖 **Words & Phrases**

suburb ⓝ a small city located near a larger one
public transportation ⓝ buses, trains, and other forms of mass transportation run by the government

subway ⓝ a train that runs underground
appealing adj pleasing; satisfying
decline ⓥ to go down; to decrease

✏️ **Summary Notes: Ashley**

Move to Suburbs

1 Encourage people to 1) _____
  • Near cities where 2) _____
  • Don't 3) _____ in cities though

2 Improve 4) _____
  • Make suburbs 5) _____
  • Cities' populations 6) _____

Brian

There is lots of empty land in some cities. For instance, there are abandoned buildings and houses in many neighborhoods. Cities should do something with the land. They can construct more housing. Or they can turn these places into parks. Doing that would make cities more comfortable and appear less populated.

📖 **Words & Phrases**

empty adj having nothing in or on something
abandoned adj left by the owner
neighborhood ⓝ a place nearby

construct ⓥ to build
appear ⓥ to seem

✏️ **Summary Notes: Brian**

Use Empty Land

1 Lots of 1) _____ in cities
  • Abandoned 2) _____

2 Do something with 3) _____
  • 4) _____ more housing
  • Turn places into 5) _____
  • Cities ➔ more 6) _____ + appear less 7) _____

Organization Review the outline and the summary notes on the previous pages and then complete each chart.

▶ **Supporting New Ideas: Making Buildings Taller**

Introduction	1 I really like _____ .
	2 I would like to _____ .
Body 1	3 Cities should _____ ,
	and they should _____ .
	4 My city _____ ,
	but _____ .
	5 They need to _____ .
Body 2	6 The reason is that _____ .
	7 This will _____ .
	8 Cities can _____ .
Conclusion	9 Then, _____ .

▶ **Supporting New Ideas: Letting People Work at Home**

Introduction	1 While Ashley and Brian _____ ,
	I _____ .
Body 1	2 Cities should _____ .
	3 This will _____ .
	4 Fewer people will _____ .
	5 So they _____ .
Body 2	6 Another benefit will be that _____ .
	7 They will _____ .
	8 As a result, _____ .
Conclusion	9 This will _____ .

Exercise 2 Follow the directions and write a response. You can refer to the outline and the summary notes.

Q Your professor is teaching a class on sociology. Write a post responding to the professor's question.

In your response you should:

- express and support your opinion
- make a contribution to the discussion

An effective response will contain at least 100 words. You will have 10 minutes to write it.

Professor
Caldwell

In our next class, we will talk about how to make people happier. Many people these days are unhappy. Their jobs, family lives, and other issues are causing them to feel this way. What do you think people should do to improve their happiness? Why do you feel that way?

📖 **Words & Phrases**

unhappy (adj) sad; not happy or pleased
job (n) the work a person does to earn money
issue (n) a problem

cause (v) to make
improve (v) to get or become better

❯ **Outline for Brainstorming**

How to Improve People's Happiness

Focus on Selves	Have More Hobbies
Reason Think of selves more	**Reason** Do activities other than watching TV and playing computer games
Example Don't think about job so much	**Example** Be active to increase level of happiness

Tucker

People should start spending more time focusing on themselves. For instance, so many people mostly think about their jobs. They get up early, work all day, and come home late at night. That is not a formula for happiness. By thinking of work less and themselves more, people will become happier.

Sheila

I believe that people need more hobbies. Instead of staying home and watching TV or playing computer games, people should do other activities. They could go hiking, read books, or learn to paint. Doing activities similar to those would increase their level of happiness.

📖 Words & Phrases

spend time [phr] to use up a certain amount of time
focus [v] to stress; to concentrate on
get up [v] to wake up
formula [n] a recipe
happiness [n] the act of being happy

hobby [n] something a person does in his or her free time
activity [n] an organized type of recreation
similar [adj] having characteristics in common
increase [v] to improve; to raise
level [n] a position on a scale

✏️ Summary Notes

Tucker
1 Spend more time focusing on selves
• Most people think about jobs
• Spend most of day at work
• Not a formula for happiness
2 Think of work less
• Think of selves more
• Become happy

Sheila
1 Need more hobbies
• Don't stay home
• Don't watch TV and play computer games
2 Do other activities
• Go hiking, read books, or learn to paint
• Increase level of happiness

_____

_____

_____

_____

_____

_____

_____

_____

_____

_____

_____

_____

_____

_____

📝 Self-Evaluation Check your response by answering the following questions.

	Yes	No
1 Did you address the professor's question?	☐	☐
2 Did you refer to the comments by the two students?	☐	☐
3 Did you express your own opinion?	☐	☐
4 Did you provide examples to support your opinion?	☐	☐
5 Did you organize your response well?	☐	☐
6 Did you use correct grammar?	☐	☐
7 Did you use correct punctuation?	☐	☐
8 Did you spell all of the words correctly?	☐	☐

Actual Test

Actual Test 01

Writing Section Directions

02-01

In this section, you will be able to demonstrate your ability to use writing to communicate in an academic environment. There will be two writing tasks.

In the first task, you will read a passage about an academic topic; you will have 3 minutes to read it. Then you will listen to a lecture about the same topic. After that, you will have **20 minutes** to combine/summarize what you have listened to and read.

For the second task, you will read an online discussion. A professor has posted a question about a topic, and some classmates have responded with their ideas. You will then write a response that contributes to the discussion. You will have **10 minutes** to write your response.

Your responses will be scored on your ability to write correctly, clearly, and coherently, as well as on your ability to respond to the questions as fully as possible.

Now, listen to the directions for the first writing task.

02-02

Writing Based on Reading and Listening Directions

For this task, you will have three minutes to read a passage about an academic topic. A clock at the top of the screen will show how much time you have to read. You may take notes while you read. You will be able to see the reading passage again when it is time for you to write. You may use your notes to help you answer the question.

You will then have **20 minutes** to write a response to a question that asks you about the relationship between the lecture you have heard and the reading passage. Try to answer the question as completely as possible using information from the reading passage and the lecture. The question does **not** ask you to express your personal opinion.

Typically, an effective response will be 150 to 225 words. Your response will be judged on the quality of your writing and on the completeness and accuracy of the content.

Now you will see the reading passage for 3 minutes. Remember that it will be available to you again while you are writing. Immediately after the reading time ends, the lecture will begin, so keep your headset on until the lecture has ended.

Task **1**

Prairie dogs are rabbit-sized rodents related to squirrels and chipmunks. These animals are native to the plains of North America. In recent decades, mostly due to human actions, their numbers have declined dramatically by up to ninety-five percent. However, there is no need to protect them because they have little value and can actually be harmful.

For one thing, prairie dogs live in places where ranchers raise cattle. In many of those places, rain is scarce. As a result, grass does not grow well at times. Prairie dogs consume large quantities of grass. The cattle that live in the same regions as prairie dogs therefore may not consume enough food when they graze. This harms cattle and causes ranchers to lose money.

A second point is that prairie dogs are not particularly important in the food chain. There are some animals, such as wolves and coyotes, that prey on them. However, prairie dogs are relatively small in size. This means that large predators cannot sustain themselves only by hunting prairie dogs. For these reasons, there is no reason for the government to make an effort to increase the prairie dog population.

02-03

Directions You have 20 minutes to plan and write your response. Your response will be judged on the basis of the quality of your writing and on how well your response presents the points in the lecture and their relationship to the reading passage. Typically, an effective response will be 150 to 225 words.

Question Summarize the points made in the lecture, being sure to explain how they cast doubt on specific points made in the reading passage.

Copy Cut Paste Word Count 0

Prairie dogs are rabbit-sized rodents related to squirrels and chipmunks. These animals are native to the plains of North America. In recent decades, mostly due to human actions, their numbers have declined dramatically by up to ninety-five percent. However, there is no need to protect them because they have little value and can actually be harmful.

For one thing, prairie dogs live in places where ranchers raise cattle. In many of those places, rain is scarce. As a result, grass does not grow well at times. Prairie dogs consume large quantities of grass. The cattle that live in the same regions as prairie dogs therefore may not consume enough food when they graze. This harms cattle and causes ranchers to lose money.

A second point is that prairie dogs are not particularly important in the food chain. There are some animals, such as wolves and coyotes, that prey on them. However, prairie dogs are relatively small in size. This means that large predators cannot sustain themselves only by hunting prairie dogs. For these reasons, there is no reason for the government to make an effort to increase the prairie dog population.

Writing for an Academic Discussion
Directions

For this task, you will read an online discussion. A professor has posted a question about a topic, and some classmates have responded with their ideas.

Write a response that contributes to the discussion. You will have **10 minutes** to write your response. It is important to use your own words in the response.

Typically, an effective essay will contain a minimum of 100 words.

Click on **Continue** to go on.

Task **2**

Your professor is teaching a class on environmental science. Write a post responding to the professor's question.

In your response you should:

- express and support your opinion
- make a contribution to the discussion

An effective response will contain at least 100 words. You will have 10 minutes to write it.

Professor Hammond

These days, the planet's environment is a major concern for people. All kinds of pollution, including ground, air, and water, are making the Earth dirty. This is resulting in numerous problems everywhere. What is the best way for people to help clean the environment? Why?

Lisa

People need to clean up after themselves. I see so many people throw trash on the ground. They should not do that. They need to use garbage cans. If they see trash somewhere, they can pick it up and throw it out. Small actions can add up to big results.

Thomas

People should start to protest against polluters. Many polluters are large factories. They send harmful smoke into the air and dump chemicals in the water. By protesting, people can force these polluters to change their ways. This will result in the environment becoming cleaner.

Copy   Cut   Paste   Word Count 0

Actual
Test 02

CONTINUE | VOLUME

02-04

Writing Section Directions

In this section, you will be able to demonstrate your ability to use writing to communicate in an academic environment. There will be two writing tasks.

In the first task, you will read a passage about an academic topic; you will have 3 minutes to read it. Then you will listen to a lecture about the same topic. After that, you will have **20 minutes** to combine/summarize what you have listened to and read.

For the second task, you will read an online discussion. A professor has posted a question about a topic, and some classmates have responded with their ideas. You will then write a response that contributes to the discussion. You will have **10 minutes** to write your response.

Your responses will be scored on your ability to write correctly, clearly, and coherently, as well as on your ability to respond to the questions as fully as possible.

Now, listen to the directions for the first writing task.

Writing Based on Reading and Listening Directions

02-05

For this task, you will have three minutes to read a passage about an academic topic. A clock at the top of the screen will show how much time you have to read. You may take notes while you read. You will be able to see the reading passage again when it is time for you to write. You may use your notes to help you answer the question.

You will then have **20 minutes** to write a response to a question that asks you about the relationship between the lecture you have heard and the reading passage. Try to answer the question as completely as possible using information from the reading passage and the lecture. The question does **not** ask you to express your personal opinion.

Typically, an effective response will be 150 to 225 words. Your response will be judged on the quality of your writing and on the completeness and accuracy of the content.

Now you will see the reading passage for 3 minutes. Remember that it will be available to you again while you are writing. Immediately after the reading time ends, the lecture will begin, so keep your headset on until the lecture has ended.

Task **1**

Large luxury cruise ships can be seen on all of the world's oceans. Many head north up the western coast of the United States and Canada. They then proceed to sail to more northern places in Alaska. While passengers enjoy these trips, the cruise ships and the passengers are harming the environment and local residents.

Cruise ships require enormous amounts of fuel to move. The oil they burn for their engines releases harmful particles that pollute the air and the water. This also kills or injures numerous marine creatures and birds. Another problem is that burning the fuel helps cause snow and ice to melt. This too can have negative effects on the Arctic environment.

During their voyages, cruise ships make frequent stops at ports in Canada and Alaska. Some of these stops are at tiny villages. In some cases, there are more passengers on the ships than there are people in the villages. The disembarking passengers often become nuisances to the locals. They consume great amounts of supplies while creating large amounts of rubbish. Rather than helping the locals, their visits cause considerable amounts of damage.

VOLUME   HELP   NEXT

Directions You have 20 minutes to plan and write your response. Your response will be judged on the basis of the quality of your writing and on how well your response presents the points in the lecture and their relationship to the reading passage. Typically, an effective response will be 150 to 225 words.

Question Summarize the points made in the lecture, being sure to explain how they challenge specific claims made in the reading passage.

Copy   Cut   Paste   Word Count   0

Large luxury cruise ships can be seen on all of the world's oceans. Many head north up the western coast of the United States and Canada. They then proceed to sail to more northern places in Alaska. While passengers enjoy these trips, the cruise ships and the passengers are harming the environment and local residents.

Cruise ships require enormous amounts of fuel to move. The oil they burn for their engines releases harmful particles that pollute the air and the water. This also kills or injures numerous marine creatures and birds. Another problem is that burning the fuel helps cause snow and ice to melt. This too can have negative effects on the Arctic environment.

During their voyages, cruise ships make frequent stops at ports in Canada and Alaska. Some of these stops are at tiny villages. In some cases, there are more passengers on the ships than there are people in the villages. The disembarking passengers often become nuisances to the locals. They consume great amounts of supplies while creating large amounts of rubbish. Rather than helping the locals, their visits cause considerable amounts of damage.

Writing for an Academic Discussion
Directions

For this task, you will read an online discussion. A professor has posted a question about a topic, and some classmates have responded with their ideas.

Write a response that contributes to the discussion. You will have **10 minutes** to write your response. It is important to use your own words in the response.

Typically, an effective essay will contain a minimum of 100 words.

Click on **Continue** to go on.

Task **2**

Your professor is teaching a class on economics. Write a post responding to the professor's question.

In your response you should:

- express and support your opinion
- make a contribution to the discussion

An effective response will contain at least 100 words. You will have 10 minutes to write it.

Professor Drago

I want to continue our discussion on consumer behavior. These days, the Internet is making it possible for people to shop from home. Online shopping has therefore become more common. Do you prefer to shop for items online? Or do you prefer to visit stores when you go shopping? Why?

VOLUME

HELP

NEXT

Leslie

I am a huge supporter of online shopping. I shop online at least once a week. I love the convenience of being able to shop from my home. I dislike dealing with crowds and pushy salespeople, too. There are no problems like that when I shop online.

Ferdinand

I have done online shopping before, but I do not care for it. I would rather visit a store to do shopping. When I shop for clothes, I feel the items and try them on. At the supermarket, I love to look at the choices and then make my selections.

Copy   Cut   Paste   Word Count   0

MEMO

How to
Master Skills for the
TOEFL® iBT
WRITING

Answers, Scripts, and Translations

Second Edition

Basic

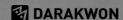

How to
Master Skills for the

Second Edition

TOEFL® iBT
WRITING   Basic

Answers, Scripts,
and Translations

DARAKWON

PART I Integrated Writing Task

Unit 01 Technology I

Exercise p.14

Reading

해석

오늘날 많은 사람들이 전자 기기로 책을 읽거나 앱을 이용하여 컴퓨터로 책을 읽는다. 사람들은 전자책의 다양한 장점 때문에 종종 전자책을 선택한다.

첫 번째 장점은 가격이다. 종이책의 가격은 지난 몇 년 동안 꾸준히 상승했다. 이로써 사람들이 여러 권의 책을 읽는 것이 어려워지고 있다. 하지만 전자책의 가격은 종이책의 절반 정도인 경우가 많고, 때때로 훨씬 더 저렴할 수 있다. 심지어 저작권이 만료된 책의 전자책 버전은 무료로 구할 수도 있다. 또한 컴퓨터로 전자책을 읽게 해 주는 대부분의 앱들은 무료로 다운로드를 할 수 있다. 그 결과 사람들은 종이책보다 전자책에서 훨씬 더 적은 비용을 쓰게 된다.

두 번째 장점은 전자책이 종이책보다 환경에 더 좋다는 점이다. 종이는 목재 펄프로 만들어지며, 이는 나무에서 나오는 것이다. 나무를, 특히 대량으로 베어 내는 것은 환경에 해가 된다. 나무는 여러 생태계에서 필수적인 존재이다. 또한 생물에게 산소를 제공해 주며 대기의 이산화탄소를 제거한다. 사람들이 종이책을 더 많이 읽을 수록 환경은 더 많은 피해를 입게 된다. 하지만 전자책은 어떠한 피해도 가져다 주지 않기 때문에 전 세계의 환경을 보호하는데 도움이 될 수 있다.

✎ Note Taking

1) half the price of paper books
2) Apps for reading e-books
3) Cut down trees
4) no harm to environment

Listening

Script 🎧 01-02

W Professor: E-books are gaining popularity these days. Proponents of e-books claim they have multiple advantages over paper books. Hmm . . . Maybe not. Let's take a closer look . . .

First, many say e-books are cheaper than paper books. Okay, uh, it's true that prices of paper books have been rising. But remember that there are many sources of cheap paper books, including used bookstores and online auction sites. Libraries, of course, provide books for free. Additionally, to read e-books, you have to purchase either an e-book reader or a computer. They can be expensive. You might also have to pay a fee to update your e-book reader. When you add everything up, I don't think e-books actually are cheaper than paper books.

Second, there are claims that e-books can help protect the environment. The reason people say this is that paper books are made from trees. That's true. But

paper is a renewable resource. Each year in many countries, millions of trees are planted to replace those that are cut down. And please be aware that e-book readers and computers cause pollution. After all, many of their parts cannot be recycled, so people discard them in landfills after finishing using them.

해석

W Professor: 전자책이 요즘 인기를 얻고 있습니다. 전자책을 선호하는 사람들은 전자책에 종이책을 뛰어넘는 여러 가지 장점이 있다고 주장을 하죠. 흠… 아닐 수도 있습니다. 보다 자세히 살펴볼게요…

첫째, 많은 사람들이 종이책보다 전자책이 저렴하다고 말을 합니다. 그래요, 어, 종이책 가격이 오르고 있는 건 사실이에요. 하지만 중고 서점 및 온라인 경매 사이트를 포함하여 저렴한 종이책을 구할 수 있는 곳들도 많습니다. 물론 도서관에서는 책을 무료로 빌려 주죠. 게다가 전자책을 읽기 위해서는 이북 리더기나 컴퓨터 중 하나를 구매해야만 해요. 이들은 비쌀 수 있습니다. 또한 이북 리더기를 업데이트하려면 비용을 내야할 수도 있어요. 모든 비용을 합산하는 경우, 이북이 종이책보다 실제로 저렴하고는 생각되지 않는군요.

둘째, 전자책이 환경 보호에 도움이 될 수 있다는 주장이 있습니다. 사람들이 그렇게 말하는 이유는 종이책이 나무로 만들어지기 때문이에요. 그건 사실입니다. 하지만 종이는 재사용이 가능한 자원이에요. 벌목된 나무들을 대체하기 위해 많은 국가에서 매년 수백만 그루의 나무가 심어지고 있습니다. 그리고 이북 리더기와 컴퓨터는 오염을 야기한다는 점을 아셔야 해요. 어쨌거나 이들의 많은 부품들은 재사용이 불가능한 것이기 때문에 사람들은 이들을 사용한 후 매립지에 버립니다.

✎ Note Taking

1) cheap paper books
2) update e-book reader
3) renewable resource
4) recycled but discarded

Comparing the Points

E-Books vs. Paper Books

Reading (Main Points)	Listening (Main Points)
E-books cost much less than paper books and can sometimes be acquired for free. In addition, people can download apps for e-readers for free.	Used bookstores and online auction sites provide paper books for cheap prices, and libraries have free books. E-book readers and computers are expensive, and upgrading apps requires a fee.
E-books also are not bad for the environment like paper books. Trees are cut down to make paper books, and cutting them down hurts numerous ecosystems.	Paper books are made from trees, which are cut down, so that hurts the environment. E-book readers and computers cause pollution when people just discard them.

Paraphrasing & Summarizing

A

1 Lots of people use electronic devices or apps to read e-books.
2 E-books cost at least fifty percent less than e-books and may be cheaper.
3 It costs nothing to download apps to read e-books in general.
4 It hurts the environment when people chop down many trees.
5 If people read many paper books, they hurt the environment a lot.

✏ Summary

Lots of people read e-books these days because of their advantages. For instance, they are cheaper than paper books. Sometimes people can get e-books for free. They also usually do not pay for apps to read e-books on computers. E-books are also better for the environment than paper books. Paper books require many trees to be cut down. This hurts the environment. E-books, meanwhile, do not hurt the environment at all.

B

1 Supporters of e-books believe they are better than paper books.
2 Used bookstores and websites can provide people with inexpensive paper books.
3 In total, paper books are less expensive than e-books.
4 Huge numbers of trees are planted each year to replace the ones chopped down.
5 People throw them away because it is not possible to recycle many of their parts.

✏ Summary

It is possible to get cheap paper books in some places. People can get them for free at libraries, too. Buying an e-book reader or computer is expensive. And people might have to pay to update e-book readers. So paper books are cheaper than e-books. Paper books are made from trees, but people plant new trees to replace the ones cut down. In addition, people usually throw away their e-book readers and computers, so this creates pollution.

Synthesizing

1 The reading passage points out that e-books can be half the price of paper books or less, but the professor remarks that there are many places to buy inexpensive paper books.

2 The author notes that there is no fee to download apps to read e-books on computers, but the professor declares that some people have to pay to update their e-book readers.
3 Whereas the reading passage claims that the cutting down of trees hurts the environment, the professor says that millions of new trees are planted annually.
4 While the author claims that e-books do not hurt the environment, the professor states that e-book readers and computers actually do create pollution.

Organization

1 The lecture and the reading passage both compare e-books with paper books.
2 The reading passage claims e-books are better than paper books, but the professor casts doubt on its arguments.
3 First, the professor points out there are high prices associated with e-books.
4 This goes against the claim in the reading passage that e-books are cheaper than paper books.
5 While the reading passage states that e-books can cost less than half the prices of paper books, the professor remarks that electronic readers and computers are expensive.
6 She also says people may have to pay a fee to update their electronic readers.
7 Second, the professor disagrees with the argument in the reading passage that e-books are better for the environment than paper books.
8 The reading passage claims that paper books require many trees to be cut down, but the professor mentions that people plant millions of new trees each year.
9 She also notes that electronic readers and computers cause pollution when people discard them.
10 In conclusion, the professor feels that e-books are not superior to paper books.

Writing

Sample Response

The lecture and the reading passage both compare e-books with paper books. The reading passage claims e-books are better than paper books, but the professor casts doubt on its arguments.

First, the professor points out there are high prices associated with e-books. This goes against the claim in the reading passage that e-books are cheaper than paper books. While the reading passage states that e-books can cost less than half the prices of paper books, the professor remarks that electronic readers and computers are expensive. She also says people may have to pay a fee to update their electronic readers.

Second, the professor disagrees with the argument in the reading passage that e-books are better for the environment than paper books. The reading passage claims that paper books require many trees to be cut down, but the professor mentions that people plant millions of new trees each year. She also notes that electronic readers and computers cause pollution when people discard them.

In conclusion, the professor feels that e-books are not superior to paper books.

해석

강의와 읽기 지문 모두 전자책과 종이책을 비교하고 있다. 읽기 지문은 전자책이 종이책보다 낫다고 주장하지만 교수는 그러한 주장에 이의를 제기한다.

첫째, 교수는 이북과 관련된 비용이 높다는 점을 지적한다. 이는 이북이 종이책보다 저렴하다는 읽기 지문의 주장과 반대되는 것이다. 읽기 지문은 전자책 가격이 종이책의 절반 이하일 수 있다고 주장하는 반면에 교수는 이북 리더기 및 컴퓨터가 비싸다는 점을 언급한다. 또한 사람들이 이북 리더기를 업데이트하려면 비용을 지불해야 할 수도 있다고 말한다.

둘째, 교수는 전자책이 종이책보다 환경에 더 좋다는 읽기 지문의 주장에 동의하지 않는다. 읽기 지문은 종이책을 만들려면 많은 나무를 베어 내야 한다고 주장하지만 교수는 매년 수백만 그루의 나무들이 새로 심어지고 있다고 언급한다. 또한 이북 리더기 및 컴퓨터를 폐기하는 경우 오염이 발생한다는 점에 주목한다.

결론적으로 교수는 전자책이 종이책보다 뛰어나지 않다고 생각한다.

Unit 02 Zoology I

Exercise p.22

Reading

해석

전 세계에서 바다거북의 개체수가 감소하고 있다. 약 650만 마리가 남아 있는데, 이는 100년 전 개체수의 2/3도 되지 않는 수치이다. 게다가 일곱 개의 주요 종 중에서 세 개의 종이 멸종 위험에 처한 것으로 생각된다.

바다거북이 줄어든 주요한 원인 중 하나는 이들이 플라스틱, 특히 비닐 봉투를 먹기 때문이다. 바다거북은 비닐 봉투를 해파리로 생각하기 때문에 이들을 먹는다. 그러면 비닐 봉투가 거북의 위에 달라붙는다. 이로써 거북들은 포만감을 느끼게 되어 먹이를 더 이상 먹지 않아서 곧 죽게 된다. 한 가지 해결 방안은 전 세계적으로 비닐 봉투의 사용을 금지하는 것이다.

바다거북이 직면하고 있는 또 다른 문제는 많은 거북들이 살고 있는 곳에서 이루어지는 어업이다. 거북들은 우연히 어망에 갇히고 낚싯줄에 걸린다. 인도네시아에서는 매년 5천 마리의 거북들이 낚싯줄에 걸려 죽는 것으로 추정된다. 이러한 어부들이 적극적으로 바다거북을 잡으려는 것은 아니다. 우연히 잡히는 것이다. 이러한 문제에 대한 한 가지 해결 방법은 많은 바다거북이 사는 곳에서 어

업을 금지시키는 것이다. 또한 거북들이 달아날 수 있는 어망을 사용할 수도 있을 것이다.

✏️ **Note Taking**

1) Consume bags
2) plastic bag usage
3) hooks on longlines
4) Prohibit fishermen

Listening

Script 🎧 01-03

M Professor: The shrinking global sea turtle population is an important issue. Sea turtles help maintain certain marine ecosystems, especially coral reefs. However, there do not seem to be any long-term solutions to this problem.

There is an enormous amount of plastic in the oceans. It kills not only sea turtles but also many other sea creatures. Some individuals have proposed banning the use of plastic products such as bags. But this simply isn't practical. The oceans are so saturated with plastic that it would take centuries for all of it to dissolve into tiny particles. Obviously, banning plastic isn't an effective immediate solution.

Fishermen are also responsible for accidentally killing many sea turtles. There have been proposals to ban fishing in certain areas and to require nets that turtles can escape from. But these solutions won't work. Most fishermen depend on their daily catches for their livelihoods. So banning them from fishing in some areas cannot happen. In addition, nets that have escape routes for turtles are expensive. The nets also let fish get out, which would reduce the number of fish fishermen catch. This means that most are reluctant to use those nets.

해석

M Professor: 전 세계적으로 바다거북의 개체수가 줄어들고 있다는 것은 중대한 문제입니다. 바다거북은 특정 해양 생태계, 특히 산호초가 유지되는데 도움을 주죠. 하지만 이러한 문제에 대한 장기적인 해결책은 없는 것으로 보입니다.

바다에는 막대한 양의 플라스틱이 존재해요. 바다거북뿐만 아니라 기타 많은 해양 동물들을 죽게 만들죠. 어떤 사람들은 비닐 봉투와 같은 플라스틱 제품의 사용을 금지하자고 주장합니다. 하지만 이는 현실적이지 않습니다. 바다는 플라스틱으로 넘쳐나기 때문에 이들이 모두 작은 입자로 분해되기까지 수 세기가 걸릴 거예요. 플라스틱 사용 금지가 효과적이고 즉각적인 해결책이 아니라는 점은 명백합니다.

또한 어부들 때문에 많은 바다거북들이 우연히 죽고 있어요. 특정 지역에서의 어업을 금지하고 거북들이 빠져나갈 수 있는 어망을 사용해야 한다는 주장도 있습니다. 하지만 이러한 해결책은 효과가 없을 거예요. 대부분의 어부들이 그날 잡은 물고기로 생계를 유지하고 있습니다. 따라서 일부 지역에서 어업을 금지시키는 일을 가능하지가 않아요. 또한 거북들을 위한 퇴로가 있는 어망은 값이 비쌉니다. 또한 이러한 어망에서는 물고기들도 빠져나갈 수 있는데, 그러면 어부들이 잡는 물고기의 수가 줄어들 것입니다. 이는 대부분의 어부들이 그러한 어망을

사용하는 것을 꺼린다는 점을 의미합니다.

1) amount of plastic
2) Oceans saturated
3) Depend on daily catches
4) let fish out

Comparing the Points

The Decline of Sea Turtle Populations

Reading (Main Points)	Listening (Main Points)
Sea turtles eat plastic bags, which get stuck in their stomachs. The turtles feel full, so they do not eat anymore and then die.	There is so much plastic in the oceans that banning plastic is not practical. Hundreds of years are required for the plastic to break down into tiny particles.
Many turtles are accidentally caught in fishermen's nets or on longlines. Fishermen could be banned from fishing in areas with many turtles and could use nets that let turtles escape.	Fishermen's livelihoods depend on their daily catches, so they cannot be stopped from fishing in some places. And nets that let turtles escape are expensive and also let fish escape, so fishermen will not use them.

Paraphrasing & Summarizing

A

1 6.5 million sea turtles remain, a sixty-six-percent decline from a century ago.
2 Sea turtles are dying because so many of them consume plastic bags.
3 The turtles are no longer hungry, so they quit eating and die.
4 Fishermen accidentally catch turtles in nets and on hooks.
5 Sea turtles could be saved if fishermen are not allowed to fish in some places.

✒️ Summary

There has been a tremendous decline in the sea turtle population in the past century. For one, the turtles eat plastic, especially bags. The bags get stuck in their stomachs, so the turtles feel full, stop eating, and die. Banning plastic bag usage could help the turtles. Fishermen also accidentally catch turtles in nets and on hooks. They could be banned from fishing in places with many turtles and could use nets that let turtles escape.

B

1 Sea turtles benefit ocean ecosystems such as coral reefs.
2 Some people believe plastic items like bags should no longer be used.
3 So much plastic is in the oceans that it will not break down for hundreds of years.
4 Some have proposed prohibiting fishing in some places and requiring specialized nets.
5 Fish can escape from the nets, so fishermen would catch fewer fish.

✒️ Summary

There are no long-term solutions to the decline in sea turtle numbers. Some people think banning plastic products would help turtles. But the oceans already have plenty of plastic. It will require centuries for the plastic in the oceans to break down. Other people want to ban fishing in certain places and to require specialized nets. But the nets are expensive and let fish escape, so fishermen will not use them.

Synthesizing

1 The author mentions that sea turtles die from eating plastic bags, and the professor says that the huge amount of plastic in the oceans kills many marine creatures.
2 While the author of the reading passage suggests banning plastic bags, the professor remarks that all of the plastic already in the oceans will not break down for centuries.
3 Although the author wants to prohibit fishing in certain areas, the professor points out that fishermen's livelihoods depend on their daily catches.
4 The reading passage author believes using nets that let turtles escape will be effective, but the professor claims fish can get out as well, so fishermen will catch fewer fish.

Organization

1 The reading passage states it is possible to stop the decline of the global sea turtle population, but the professor challenges those claims.
2 First, the professor points out that there is already a huge amount of plastic in the oceans.
3 In fact, there is so much plastic that it will not disappear from the oceans for centuries.
4 The professor therefore refutes the claim in the reading passage that banning plastic bags will help sea turtles.
5 Second, the professor discusses fishermen who accidentally kill sea turtles.

6 He says banning them from fishing in some places will not work because their livelihoods depend on fishing every day.

7 He also remarks that fishermen will not buy nets that let turtles escape.

8 The nets are too expensive and let fish escape, too.

9 In this way, he challenges the claim that forcing fishermen to act differently will help sea turtles.

10 The professor uses these two arguments to prove the claims in the reading passage will not work.

Writing

Sample Response

The reading passage states it is possible to stop the decline of the global sea turtle population, but the professor challenges those claims.

First, the professor points out that there is already a huge amount of plastic in the oceans. In fact, there is so much plastic that it will not disappear from the oceans for centuries. The professor therefore refutes the claim in the reading passage that banning plastic bags will help sea turtles.

Second, the professor discusses fishermen who accidentally kill sea turtles. He says banning them from fishing in some places will not work because their livelihoods depend on fishing every day. He also remarks that fishermen will not buy nets that let turtles escape. The nets are too expensive and let fish escape, too. In this way, he challenges the claim that forcing fishermen to act differently will help sea turtles.

The professor uses these two arguments to prove the claims in the reading passage will not work.

해석

읽기 지문은 전 세계적인 바다거북의 개체수 감소를 막을 수 있다고 주장하지만 교수는 그러한 주장을 반박한다.

첫째, 교수는 이미 바다에 막대한 양의 플라스틱이 존재한다는 점을 지적한다. 실제로 플라스틱이 너무 많기 때문에 이들은 수 세기 동안 바다에서 사라지지 않을 것이다. 따라서 교수는 비닐 봉투의 사용 금지가 바다거북에게 도움이 될 것이라는 읽기 지문의 주장을 반박한다.

둘째, 교수는 의도하지 않게 바다거북을 죽이고 있는 어부에 대해 논의한다. 그는 이들의 생계가 하루 어업량에 달려 있기 때문에 일부 지역에서 어업을 금지시키는 것은 효과가 없을 것이라고 말한다. 또한 거북들이 빠져나갈 수 있는 어망을 어부들이 구입하지 않으려 할 것이라고 언급한다. 그러한 어망은 값이 비싸며 물고기를 또한 가두어 놓지 못할 것이다. 이로써 그는 어부들의 행위를 변화시키는 것이 바다거북에게 도움이 될 것이라는 주장을 반박한다.

교수는 그러한 두 가지 논점을 통해 읽기 지문의 주장이 효과가 없을 것이라는 점을 입증하고 있다.

Exercise p.30

Reading

해석

거짓말 탐지기는 어떤 사람이 거짓말을 하고 있는지 알려 주는 기기이다. 이는 사람의 심박수, 혈압, 그리고 호흡 패턴을 측정한다. 경찰이 범죄 용의자를 심문할 때 종종 이를 사용한다. 하지만 법정은 그러한 결과를 증거로 받아들이지 않는 경우가 많다. 하지만 이러한 상황은 향후에 바뀔 수도 있다.

거짓말 탐지기로 심문을 받는 사람이 결과를 조종할 수 있는 방법을 찾아낼 수도 있다. 호흡과 심박수를 신체적으로 통제하는 법을 익힐 수 있다. 하지만 새로운 거짓말 탐지기는 뇌 활동을 측정한다. 사람들이 거짓말을 하면 뇌의 특정 영역이 보다 활동적이 된다. 뇌 활동을 통제하는 것은 사실상 불가능하다. 따라서 이러한 새로운 거짓말 탐지기는 사람들이 거짓말로 진실을 감추는 것을 막을 수 있다.

많은 국가의 경우 거짓말 탐지 결과는 형사 사건에서 증거로 사용되지 않는다. 실제 범죄자가 자신의 신체를 통제할 수도 있고, 무고한 사람들에게서 유죄인 결과가 나타날 수도 있다. 그 이유는 테스트를 받을 때 너무 긴장을 하기 때문이다. 따라서 거짓말 탐지기가 사실을 말하는 상황에서도 이를 거짓으로 잘못 판명하게 된다. 뇌 활동을 측정하는 새로운 거짓말 탐지기는 이러한 문제를 완화시킬 것이다. 따라서 향후에는 많은 법정에서 거짓말 탐지기의 결과가 증거로서 채택될 것이다.

Note Taking

1) control results
2) control brain activity
3) produce guilty results
4) reduce problems

Listening

Script 🎧 01-04

M Professor: There are some new lie detectors different from the old ones. The new ones measure brain activity. This breakthrough has led people to believe lie detectors are now unbeatable. Nothing could be further from the truth.

To measure brain activity, the subject's head is connected to sensors. To see the results, the person must be placed in an MRI machine. It maps brain functions during questions. However, there's evidence that people can control their brain activity during tests. A study done at the University of Plymouth in England in 2019 proved this. Subjects tested utilized mental defenses to hide their lies. They reduced the detector's ability to tell if they were lying by twenty percent.

Another issue to consider is that every person's brain is different. A standard test of the brain for lying may not work on everyone. Some people may show brain activity when they lie whereas others may not. There's also evidence that seasoned criminals are so used to lying that there's no unusual brain activity when they tell falsehoods. As a result, the results are not yet being used as evidence by courts . . . and maybe they never will be.

해석

M Professor: 기존 탐지기들과 다른 새로운 거짓말 탐지기가 나왔습니다. 새로운 탐지기는 뇌 활동을 측정해요. 이 획기적인 발명으로 사람들은 거짓말 탐지기가 이제 무적이 되었다고 생각하고 있어요. 하지만 전혀 그렇지가 않습니다.

뇌 활동을 측정할 때 대상자의 머리는 센서와 연결됩니다. 결과를 보기 위해서는 그 사람이 MRI 기기에 들어가야 하죠. 그러면 질문을 하는 동안 뇌 기능이 측정됩니다. 하지만 사람들이 테스트를 받는 동안 뇌 활동을 통제할 수 있다는 증거가 존재합니다. 2019년 영국의 플리머스 대학에서 이루어진 한 연구에서 이러한 점이 입증되었어요. 실험 대상자들은 정신 방어를 활용하여 자신의 거짓말을 감추었습니다. 거짓말을 탐지하는 탐지기의 능력을 20% 감소시켰죠.

생각해야 할 또 다른 문제는 모든 사람의 뇌가 다르다는 점이에요. 거짓말하는 뇌에 대한 표준 검사는 일부 사람들에게 효과가 없을 수도 있습니다. 어떤 사람들은 거짓말을 할 때 뇌 활동이 나타나지만 그렇지 않은 사람들도 있을 수 있어요. 또한 노련한 범죄자들은 거짓말에 익숙하기 때문에 거짓을 말하는 경우에도 특이한 뇌 활동이 나타나지 않는다는 증거가 있죠. 따라서 그러한 결과는 아직 법정에서 증거로 사용될 수 없으며… 앞으로도 결코 사용되지 않을 수도 있습니다.

Note Taking

1) MRI machine
2) twenty percent
3) Standard tests
4) Seasoned criminals

Comparing the Points

New Lie Detectors

Reading (Main Points)	Listening (Main Points)
People can control their breathing and heart rate when they take lie detector tests. But new lie detectors measure brain activity, which people cannot control.	An MRI machine measures brain activity during the test. But a 2019 university study showed that people could use mental defenses to hide their lies effectively.
Criminals can control their bodies, but innocent people may get nervous, so the lie detector shows they are lying. New lie detectors will reduce the likelihood of this happening.	People have different brains, so standard tests might not work for everyone. Seasoned criminals also lie so much that they show no unusual brain activity when they lie.

Paraphrasing & Summarizing

A

1 A lie detector is a tool that can find liars.

2 Some people can control the results of their lie detector tests.

3 Most people have no control over their brain activity.

4 Nonguilty people might product negative results whereas criminals can control their bodies.

5 By mistake, lie detectors show that honest people were telling lies.

Summary

Lie detector results are not accepted in most courts. The reason is that some people can control their bodies. But new lie detectors measure brain activity, which almost nobody can control. In addition, criminals can control their bodies while innocent people get nervous during tests. This makes lie detectors have wrong results. New lie detectors will reduce the likelihood of this happening though. As a result, courts will accept their results in the future.

B

1 A new development has made people think lie detectors make no mistakes.

2 Yet people have been shown to be able to control their brains when tested.

3 The lie detector's effectiveness was lowered by one-fifth.

4 Not all people exhibit any brain activity when they tell lies.

5 People who are criminals lie so much that their brains show no unique activity when they lie.

Summary

Some people think that new lie detectors are unbeatable, but they are wrong. An MRI machine measures brain activity during tests. However, a 2019 university study showed that people could use mental defenses effectively to hide their lies. In addition, people's brains are different, so some may show no brain activity when they lie. Criminals lie so much that they exhibit no special brain activity, too. So the results may never be used in courts.

Synthesizing

1 While the reading passage argues that most people cannot control their brain activity, the professor argues that people can do that during tests.

2 In contrast to the claim that new lie detectors do not let people hide their lies, the professor shows that people can use mental defenses to lie during lie detector tests.

3 The author writes that criminals can control their bodies while innocent people cannot, but the professor states that standard tests are not effective for everyone.

4 Whereas the author of the reading passage believes courts will accept the results of new lie detectors, the professor thinks they may never be accepted.

Organization

1 In the reading passage, the writer argues that new lie detectors will probably be accepted by courts soon.

2 However, the professor disagrees with the points made in the reading passage.

3 The professor first discusses how the new lie detector maps brain functions.

4 He then mentions a university study in which people hid their lies by using mental defenses.

5 This made the new lie detectors less reliable.

6 He therefore shows that the argument in the reading passage that people cannot lie to lie detectors is not true.

7 Next, the professor points out that everyone's brain is different, so the lie detector may not work for some people.

8 He also remarks that criminals lie so much that their brain activity is not unusual when they are lying.

9 In this way, he shows that the writer's argument that new lie detectors can measure brain activity well is not accurate.

10 The professor therefore casts doubt on the arguments made in the reading passage.

Writing

Sample Response

In the reading passage, the writer argues that new lie detectors will probably be accepted by courts soon. However, the professor disagrees with the points made in the reading passage.

The professor first discusses how the new lie detector maps brain functions. He then mentions a university study in which people hid their lies by using mental defenses. This made the new lie detectors less reliable. He therefore shows that the argument in the reading passage that people cannot lie to lie detectors is not true.

Next, the professor points out that everyone's brain is different, so the lie detector may not work for some people. He also remarks that criminals lie so much that their brain activity is not unusual when they are lying. In this way, he shows that the writer's argument that new lie detectors can measure brain activity well is not accurate.

The professor therefore casts doubt on the arguments made in the reading passage.

해석

읽기 지문에서 글쓴이는 아마도 새로운 거짓말 탐지기가 곧 법정에서 받아들여질 것이라고 주장한다. 하지만 교수는 읽기 지문에서 제시된 논점에 동의하지 않는다.

교수는 먼저 새로운 거짓말 탐지기가 어떻게 뇌 기능을 측정하는지에 대해 논의한다. 그런 다음 사람들이 정신 방어를 이용하여 거짓말을 숨겼던 한 대학교의 연구를 언급한다. 이로써 새로운 거짓말 탐지기의 신뢰도가 떨어지게 되었다. 따라서 그는 사람들이 거짓말 탐지기에 거짓을 말할 수 없다는 읽기 지문의 주장이 사실이 아니라는 점을 보여 준다.

다음으로 교수는 모든 사람들의 뇌가 다르기 때문에 거짓말 탐지기가 일부 사람들에게 효과가 없을 수도 있다는 점을 지적한다. 또한 범죄자들은 거짓말을 너무 많이 하기 때문에 이들이 거짓말을 하는 경우에도 그들의 뇌 활동이 특이하지 않다는 점을 언급한다. 이런 식으로 그는 거짓말 탐지기가 뇌 활동을 제대로 측정할 수 있다는 글쓴이의 주장이 정확하지 않다는 점을 보여 준다.

따라서 교수는 읽기 지문에서 제기된 주장에 의문을 제기한다.

Unit 04 Astronomy

Exercise p.38

Reading

해석

화성 탐사가 현재 미국 항공 우주국인 NASA에 의해 계획되고 있다. 탐사와 관련된 주요 관심사 중 하나는 화성의 어디에 착륙을 해야 하는가이다. 두 개의 지점, 즉 적도 및 극지방 중 한 곳이 제안되었다. 보다 나은 선택은 화성의 적도 부근 어딘가가 될 것이다.

장기간의 화성 탐사가 성공하려면 반드시 물을 찾아야 한다. 어찌되었든 물은 인간의 생존과 식물의 성장에 필수적인 것이다. 과학자들은 적도 인근의 잠재적인 착륙 지점 여덟 곳을 정확히 제시했다. 이러한 지점은 그 표면 아래에 물이 있다는 증거를 보여 주기 때문에 적합하다. 굴착을 하면 우주비행사들이 물을 끌어 올릴 수 있을 것이다.

적도는 또한 화성의 다른 어떤 지역보다 날씨가 따뜻하다. 그곳의 여름 기온은 섭씨 20도 정도이다. 그와 대조적으로 극지방 인근의 기온은 섭씨 영하 100도를 기록한 적이 있다. 적도에서는 또한 낮 시간이 길며 극지방에서보다 햇빛이 더 많이 든다. 화상 탐사에서는 태양열 발전에 의지하여 기기를 작동하게 될 것이다. 극지방에서는 하루에 받을 수 있는 햇빛의 양이 제한되어 있기 때문에 태양열 발전이 어렵다.

Note Taking

1) potential landing sites
2) beneath the surface
3) 20 degrees Celsius
4) solar power

Listening

Script 🎧 01-05

W Professor: Members of the space community have long dreamed of establishing a permanent base on Mars. Where to do that is an important consideration. The most favorable location appears to be the poles.

The Martian north and south poles both have permanent ice caps of frozen water on the surface. Either would provide a long-term water supply for astronauts. While the equator has water, it will not be easy to obtain there. The water is located underground, and astronauts will need to find it and then drill for it. There's also no guarantee they will find water where they land at the equator. The poles are therefore a safer bet for a Mars base.

Temperature fluctuations at the equator are another problem. The temperature can range from twenty degrees Celsius in the day to far into the negatives at night. This fluctuation would be hard on the machinery. The metal would expand and contract and possibly break down. At the poles, the temperature is steady pretty much all day. The equator would be better for capturing sunlight for solar power. Yet a Mars base at a pole could use a nuclear generator to produce all the power it needs.

해석

W Professor: 우주 탐사와 관련된 일을 하는 사람들은 오랫동안 화성에 영구적인 기지를 건설하는 것을 꿈꿔 왔습니다. 어디에서 그렇게 해야 하는지가 중요한 고려 사항이죠. 가장 적합한 곳은 극지방으로 보입니다.

화성의 북극과 남극의 지표면에는 모두 얼음으로 이루어진 영구적인 만년설이 존재해요. 둘 중 어느 곳이라도 우주 비행사들에게 장기간 동안 물을 공급해 줄 것입니다. 적도에도 물이 있지만, 그곳에서 물을 얻기는 쉽지 않을 거예요. 물이 지하에 있어서 우주 비행사들은 물을 찾아낸 후 굴착을 해서 물을 얻어야 하죠. 또한 착륙한 적도 지점에서 물을 찾게 될 것이라는 점도 보장되지 않습니다. 따라서 화성 기지 장소로서는 극지방이 더 안전한 선택인 것이죠.

또 다른 문제로 적도의 기온 변화가 있습니다. 낮에는 섭씨 20도였다가 밤에는 기온이 뚝 떨어져 마이너스가 될 수도 있어요. 이러한 변화는 기기에 무리를 줄 것입니다. 금속이 팽창과 수축을 하다가 파손될 수도 있는 것이죠. 극지방에서는 하루 종일 기온이 꽤 일정한 상태로 유지됩니다. 적도에서 태양열 발전에 필요한 태양빛을 얻기가 더 좋을 거예요. 하지만 극지방의 화성 기지는 원자력 발전기를 사용해서 필요한 모든 전력을 생산해 낼 수도 있습니다.

✏ Note Taking

1) Permanent ice caps
2) Long-term water supply
3) Temperature fluctuations
4) break down

Comparing the Points

Mars Mission: Equator vs. Pole

Reading (Main Points)	Listening (Main Points)
There are eight potential sites to land at the equator. They should have water beneath the surface that astronauts can drill down to pump out.	There is frozen water at the permanent ice caps at the poles, which will give astronauts a long-term water supply. At the equator, astronauts might drill but not find any water.
The equator can get as warm as twenty degrees Celsius, making it much warmer than the poles. It has more access to sunlight, so astronauts can use solar power to operate machinery.	At the equator, there are temperature fluctuations, which will be hard on machinery and make it break down. At a pole, nuclear energy could be used to produce power.

Paraphrasing & Summarizing

A

1 NASA is planning to send some astronauts to Mars.
2 The sites are ideal since they are believed to have underground water.
3 Astronauts can dig into the ground and extract the water.
4 However, the temperature can get extremely cold at the Martian poles.
5 There is not much sunlight at the poles, so little solar power can be produced.

⊘ Summary

NASA is planning to send astronauts to Mars and should land at the equator. There are eight spots around the equator that should have underground water. Astronauts can drill into the ground and then pump out the water to survive. The temperature at the equator can be twenty degrees Celsius whereas it is extremely cold at the poles. The equator also gets more sunlight, so it will be possible to operate machinery with solar power.

B

1 People involved in space have wanted to visit Mars for a long time.
2 There is ice at the permanent ice caps at both of the Martian poles.
3 Although the equator has water, accessing it will be hard.

4   The high temperature is twenty degrees Celsius while the low is far below zero.

5   Astronauts at the poles could use nuclear power for their electricity needs.

Summary

A mission to Mars should visit one of the poles. Astronauts can get long-term access to water at the permanent ice caps there. There is water at the equator, but getting it will be difficult. Astronauts might dig but find nothing. The temperature fluctuates too much at the equator. That will make equipment expand and contract and then break down. Astronauts at a pole can generate electricity by using nuclear power.

Synthesizing

1   Although the author states that the sites show evidence of underground water, the professor points out there is frozen water at both the north and south poles.

2   While the reading passage notes that astronauts can drill for water underground, the professor says that they might not find any water at the equator.

3   Both the reading passage and the professor acknowledge the temperature can get up to twenty degrees Celsius, but the professor adds that nighttime temperatures are extremely cold.

4   Whereas the author of the reading passage mentions that solar power can be used, the professor argues in favor of using a nuclear generator to make power at a pole.

Organization

1   The reading passage and the lecture are both about possible sites for a base on Mars.

2   However, the professor disagrees with the selected location by the author of the reading passage.

3   To begin with, the professor states that the north and south poles of Mars have plenty of frozen water on the surface for astronauts to use.

4   Then, she says that water at the equator is underground, which will make it hard to find and drill for.

5   This challenges the argument made in the reading passage that the equator is the better place for a Mars mission.

6   After that, the professor discusses the temperatures at the poles and the equator.

7   The temperature at the poles is constant, so that will be good for the machinery.

8   The temperature at the equator fluctuates too much, which will make the machinery break down.

9   The professor therefore contradicts the argument that the equator will be better because of its warmer weather.

10 In her lecture, the professor effectively challenges the arguments made in the reading passage.

Writing

Sample Response

The reading passage and the lecture are both about possible sites for a base on Mars. However, the professor disagrees with the selected location by the author of the reading passage.

To begin with, the professor states that the north and south poles of Mars have plenty of frozen water on the surface for astronauts to use. Then, she says that water at the equator is underground, which will make it hard to find and drill for. This challenges the argument made in the reading passage that the equator is the better place for a Mars mission.

After that, the professor discusses the temperatures at the poles and the equator. The temperature at the poles is constant, so that will be good for the machinery. The temperature at the equator fluctuates too much, which will make the machinery break down. The professor therefore contradicts the argument that the equator will be better because of its warmer weather.

In her lecture, the professor effectively challenges the arguments made in the reading passage.

해석

읽기 지문과 강의 모두 화성에 기지를 세울 수 있는 장소에 관한 것이다. 하지만 교수는 읽기 지문의 작가가 선택한 장소에 대해 다른 의견을 제시한다.

먼저 교수는 화성의 북극과 남극 표면에 우주 비행사들이 이용할 수 있는 다량의 얼음이 존재한다고 주장한다. 그런 다음 적도에 있는 물은 지하에 있기 때문에 이를 찾아 굴착해서 얻기가 힘들 것이라고 말한다. 이는 적도가 화성 탐사에 보다 적합한 장소라는 읽기 지문의 주장과 반대되는 것이다.

그 후 교수는 극지방과 적도의 기온에 대해 논의한다. 극지방의 기온은 일정한 편으로, 이는 기기에 도움이 될 것이다. 적도의 기온은 크게 변하는데, 이로 인해 기기들이 파손될 것이다. 따라서 교수는 따뜻한 날씨 때문에 적도가 더 적합할 것이라는 주장을 반박한다.

강의에서 교수는 읽기 지문에서 제기된 논점에 대해 효과적으로 반박하고 있다.

Unit 05 Education

Exercise ·· p.46

Reading

해석

초등학교 학생들에게 음악을 가르치는 것에 관한 논쟁이 계속되고 있다. 일부 사람들은 필요하다고 생각하지만 그렇지 않다고 생각하는 사람들도 있다. 전체적으로 볼 때 음악 교육에는 장점보다 단점이 더 많다.

먼저 적절하게 음악을 가르치기 위해서는 많은 수업 시간이 요구된다. 하지만 이 시간은 보다 중요한 스킬, 즉 수학과 언어와 같은 스킬을 공부하는데 사용될 수 있다. 음악은 많은 사람들이 졸업 후에 결코 다시 사용하지 않는 스킬이다. 반면에 수학, 읽기, 과학, 그리고 외국어 수업에서 얻은 지식은 평생에 걸쳐 학생들에게 도움을 준다. 따라서 음악을 배우는 것은 학생들에게 귀중한 시간을 낭비하는 일이다.

비용 또한 음악 교육에 문제가 된다. 정규 초등학교 교사들은 학생들에게 다양한 과목을 가르친다. 하지만 음악은 특별한 스킬을 요구하기 때문에 그들이 음악을 가르칠 수는 없다. 따라서 학교들은 전임 음악 교사를 고용해야 한다. 추가적인 비용이 든다는 점에서 음악 교육은 그다지 비용 효과적이지 못하다. 악기 또한 값이 비쌀 수 있다. 가격이 천 달러 이상인 악기들도 있다. 학부모들이 이러한 악기 비용을 부담할 것으로 생각되지만, 많은 학부모들은 이를 감당할 수가 없다. 이로 인해 초등학생이 음악을 배우려면 너무 많은 비용이 든다.

✏ Note Taking

1) after graduate
2) math, reading, science
3) full-time music teachers
4) Musical instruments

Listening

Script 🎧 01-06

W Professor: It's unfortunate that so many people are opposed to elementary school students learning music. I believe it's a wonderful idea. Let me tell you why.

Music is a language all on its own. People can best benefit from learning music by studying it at an early age. Learning how to make music by reading sheet music and playing instruments has numerous long-term benefits. For instance, young students begin to recognize patterns. These patterns are present in languages and mathematics as well. By learning music, students can reinforce their skills in other subjects. The ability to understand music can last a lifetime, too.

Now, uh, I've heard the argument that music classes are too expensive. Yet these costs can be offset in various ways. Schools can hire part-time or retired music teachers instead of full-time ones. Additionally, parents with musical talents can volunteer to teach. It's also cheap simply to rent musical instruments rather than to buy them outright. And many families have musical instruments at home. Students can take them to school for class and then bring them back home to practice at night.

해석

W Professor: 초등학교 학생들이 음악을 배우는 것을 그처럼 많은 사람들이 반대하다니 안타깝습니다. 저는 그것이 훌륭한 아이디어라고 생각해요. 그 이유를 말씀드리죠.

음악 그 자체가 하나의 언어입니다. 사람들은 어린 나이에 음악을 배움으로써 가장 큰 혜택을 수 누릴 수 있어요. 악보를 읽고 악기를 사용하여 연주하는 법을 배우면 장기적으로 많은 혜택을 누리게 되죠. 예를 들어 어린 학생들은 패턴을 인식하기 시작합니다. 이러한 패턴은 언어와 수학에도 존재하는 것이에요. 음악을 배움으로써 학생들은 다른 과목의 스킬들을 강화시킬 수가 있습니다. 또한 음악을 이해하는 능력은 평생 지속될 수 있습니다.

자, 어, 음악 수업의 비용이 너무 많이 든다는 주장은 저도 들었어요. 하지만 그러한 비용은 다양한 방식으로 상쇄시킬 수 있어요. 학교측은 전임 음악 교사 대신 시간제 교사나 퇴직한 음악 교사를 고용할 수 있어요. 게다가 음악적인 재능을 가지고 있는 부모들이 자원봉사로 음악을 가르칠 수도 있죠. 또한 악기를 구입하는 대신 악기를 대여하면 비용이 적게 듭니다. 그리고 많은 가정들이 집에 악기를 두고 있어요. 학생들은 학교에 악기를 가져와 수업을 하고 그 후에는 악기를 다시 집에 가져가서 밤에 연습을 하면 되는 것이죠.

✏ Note Taking

1) sheet music
2) reinforce skills
3) retired music teachers
4) musical instruments

Comparing the Points

Teaching Music to Elementary School Students

Reading (Main Points)	Listening (Main Points)
It takes time to teach music, but that time could be used for other subjects, such as math and languages. In addition, many students do not use their music skills after they graduate, but they use knowledge learned in other classes.	People can benefit from learning to read sheet music and to play musical instruments at a young age. They also learn to recognize patterns and reinforce their skills in various subjects.
Schools must hire full-time music teachers, which is not cost effective. Students also need musical instruments, but they are expensive, so many parents cannot afford them.	Schools can hire part-time or retired music teachers or get musically talented parents to volunteer. Families can also rent instruments or use ones that they already have.

Paraphrasing & Summarizing

A

1 There are more drawbacks than benefits to teaching music.

2 Most people will not use their music skills after they finish school.

3 However, students will use the knowledge they learn in other classes for as long as they live.

4 Children's instructors teach many different classes.

5 Students' parents should pay for the instruments but do not have enough money.

Summary

There are more disadvantages than advantages to teaching elementary school students music. For instance, most students do not use music after they finish school. But they use skills learned in other classes for the rest of their lives. This makes learning music a waste of time. Schools also need to hire full-time music teachers, which can be expensive. And many parents do not have enough money to buy musical instruments for their children.

B

1 It is too bad people do not want young students to study music.

2 There are long-term advantages to learn to read music and to play music.

3 Students can use music to make other skills better.

4 Schools can employ part-time teachers or ones that no longer work.

5 Renting instruments is cheaper than paying to purchase them.

Summary

Teaching music to elementary school students is a wonderful idea. Students can gain by learning to read sheet music and to play instruments. They can also use music to reinforce the skills they have in other subjects. Schools can hire part-time or retired teachers or have parents with musical talents volunteer instead of hiring expensive full-time teachers. They can also save money by renting instruments or by using instruments they have at their homes.

Synthesizing

1 Whereas the reading passage claims many students will not use their music skills after they graduate, the professor states that there are long-term benefits to reading sheet music and to playing instruments.

2 The reading passage argues that music is a waste of time for students, but the professor states that students can use music to reinforce their skills in other subjects.

3 Although the author of the reading passage believes schools need to hire full-time music teachers, the professor remarks that schools can use part-time or retired teachers instead.

4 The reading passage mentions that many parents cannot afford to buy instruments, yet the professor points out that renting them is cheaper.

Organization

1 Both the lecture and the reading passage are concerned about teaching music to elementary school students.

2 The professor supports this activity by pointing out benefits such as teaching students to read sheet music and to recognize patterns.

3 She mentions that these skills are helpful to students when they student math and languages.

4 She therefore casts doubt on the claim in the reading passage that learning music is a waste of time for students.

5 The professor then discusses the costs involved.

6 Instead of hiring full-time teachers as the reading passage suggests, she wants to hire part-time instructors.

7 She also notes that parents can volunteer to teach music.

8 Then, she says that renting musical instruments is cheaper than buying them, which is mentioned by the author of the reading passage.

9 She adds that many families already have musical instruments which their children can use.

10 By bringing up those points, the professor casts doubt on the points that are made in the reading passage.

Writing

Sample Response

Both the lecture and the reading passage are concerned about teaching music to elementary school students.

The professor supports this activity by pointing out benefits such as teaching students to read sheet music and to recognize patterns. She mentions that these skills are helpful to students when they student math and languages. She therefore casts doubt on the claim in the reading passage that learning music is a waste of time for students.

The professor then discusses the costs involved. Instead of hiring full-time teachers as the reading passage suggests, she wants to hire part-time instructors. She also notes that parents can volunteer to teach music. Then, she says that renting musical instruments is cheaper than buying them, which is mentioned by the author of the reading passage. She adds that many families already have musical instruments which their children can use.

By bringing up those points, the professor casts doubt on the points that are made in the reading passage.

해석

강의와 읽기 지문 모두 초등학교 학생들에게 음악을 가르치는 것에 관한 내용을 다루고 있다.

교수는 학생들이 악보를 읽고 패턴을 인식하는 것을 배우는 것과 같은 혜택들을 지적하면서 그러한 교육 활동을 지지한다. 그녀는 학생들이 수학과 언어를 공부할 때 이러한 스킬이 학생들에게 도움이 된다고 언급한다. 따라서 그녀는 음악 교육이 학생들에게 시간 낭비라고 한 읽기 지문의 주장에 의구심을 제기한다.

그런 다음 교수는 관련 비용에 대해 논의한다. 읽기 지문의 제안과 같이 전임 교사를 고용하는 대신 그녀는 시간제 교사의 고용을 지지한다. 또한 부모들이 자원봉사로 음악을 가르칠 수도 있다고 언급한다. 그런 다음 그녀는 악기 대여 비용이 구입 비용보다 더 저렴하다고 말한다. 그녀는 덧붙여서 아이들이 사용할 수 있는 악기들이 이미 많은 가정에 구비되어 있다고 말한다.

이러한 점들을 지적하면서 교수는 읽기 지문에서 제시한 논점들에 의구심을 제기한다.

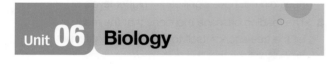

Unit 06 Biology

Exercise p.54

Reading

해석

낙우송은 전형적으로 늪 및 기타 습지에서 자라는 나무이다. 낙우송은 독특한 뿌리로 유명한데, 이들의 뿌리는 수직으로 자라서 물 밖으로 나오며, 때때로 기근이라고 불린다. 이들 뿌리는 두 가지 중요한 기능을 수행한다. 산소를 흡수하는 것과 나무를 땅에 고정시키는 것이다.

식물들이 광합성을 통해 양분을 얻기 위해서는 산소가 필요하다. 늪과 같은 습지에 사는 식물들은 종종 수중에 뿌리가 존재하는데, 이로써 공기로부터 산소를 흡수하는 일이 어려워진다. 하지만 낙우송의 뿌리는 수위선 위로 자란다. 이로써 낙우송은 대기로부터 쉽게 산소를 흡수할 수 있다. 많은 산소를 흡수하기 때문에 낙우송은 습지에 사는 다른 나무들보다 더 높고 크게 자란다.

낙우송은 또한 스스로를 토양에 고정시켜야 한다. 습지는 보통 물로 덮여 있기 때문에 토양이 무른 편이다. 습지의 식물들은 뿌리를 더 많이 자라게 함으로써 땅에 더 단단하게 고정되어 있을 수 있다. 이로써 나무가 강풍이나 홍수로 쓰러지지 않게 된다. 나무의 뿌리는 또한 습지의 물을 흡수하는데, 이로 인해 땅이 덜 무르게 된다. 이는 또 다시 토양 침식을 예방해 준다.

1) photosynthesis
2) waterline
3) high winds
4) soil erosion

Listening

Script 🎧 01-07

W Professor: This . . . is a picture of a bald cypress tree. Please note its distinct roots, which grow above the water. These roots are called knees because they resemble human knees. Let's examine the functions of these roots . . .

Some botanists claim the vertical roots enable the tree to absorb more oxygen from the air than other trees. Well . . . that's not precisely true. You see, uh, some bald cypress trees grow on dry land and have no aboveground roots. A comparison was made between bald cypresses growing on dry land and in wetlands. The study determined that wetland cypress trees had no significantly higher levels of oxygen.

Another claim is that the vertical roots of the trees in wetlands help anchor them to the soil. However, these roots grow up and above the soil and are not actually in the ground beneath the water. There are horizontal roots beneath the soil that act as anchors though. They spread out under the soil and keep the tree in the ground. The vertical roots grow from these horizontal roots. Perhaps the vertical roots provide better stability for the horizontal roots, but more studies are needed to determine that.

해석

W Professor: 이것이… 낙우송의 사진이에요. 독특한 뿌리에 주목해야 하는데, 뿌리가 물 위로 자라나죠. 이 뿌리는 인간의 무릎과 비슷하게 생겼기 때문에 기근이라고 불립니다. 이들 뿌리의 기능을 살펴보도록 할게요…

몇몇 식물학자들은 수직근 덕분에 이 나무가 다른 나무에 비해 대기에서 보다 많은 산소를 흡수한다고 주장해요. 음… 정확히는 그렇지가 않습니다. 아시다시피, 어, 일부 낙우송들은 건조한 지역에서 자라는데, 그 뿌리가 지면 위로 올라오지 않아요. 건조한 지역에서 자라는 낙우성과 습지에서 자라는 낙우송에 대한 비교가 이루어졌습니다. 이 연구에서는 습지의 낙우송이 의미 있는 정도로 더 많은 양의 산소를 가지고 있지는 않다는 점이 밝혀졌어요.

또 다른 주장은 습지에서 수직으로 자라는 뿌리가 이 나무들이 토양에 고정되는 것을 돕는다는 것입니다. 하지만 이들의 뿌리는 성장해서 토양 위로 자라난 것이지 실제로 물속의 땅에 박혀 있지는 않아요. 대신 토양 아래에 고정 장치로 기능하는 수평근이 존재합니다. 이들이 토양 아래에서 퍼져 나가 나무를 땅에 고정시키는 것이죠. 수직근은 이러한 수평근에서 자라납니다. 아마도 수직근이 수평근의 안정성을 높여 줄 수도 있지만, 이러한 점을 밝혀내기 위해서는 더 많은 연구가 필요합니다.

1) wetlands
2) oxygen levels
3) Vertical roots
4) Horizontal roots

Comparing the Points

Functions of Bald Cypress Tree Roots

Reading (Main Points)	Listening (Main Points)
Bald cypress roots grow above the waterline, so they can absorb more oxygen for photosynthesis. Because they take in so much oxygen, they grow taller and larger than other wetland trees.	Bald cypress trees grow on dry land and in wetlands. A comparison of trees showed that ones growing in wetlands did not have significantly higher levels of oxygen.
Bald cypress tree roots grow above the ground, so they can anchor the tree to the ground better. Their roots absorb water, too, so they help prevent soil erosion.	The horizontal roots that grow above the soil do not act as anchors. The vertical roots that grow underground spread out, so they anchor the tree to the soil.

Paraphrasing & Summarizing

A

1 The tree's roots are called knees and grow upward out of the water.
2 Plants make food by using oxygen during photosynthesis.
3 Because it gets more oxygen, it is bigger than other trees in swamps.
4 Since they have more roots, wetland trees can stay in the ground better.
5 The soil is more compact because the roots take in water from the wetlands.

⊘ Summary

The bald cypress tree has distinct roots growing out of the ground and called knees. These roots help the tree undergo photosynthesis since they absorb so much oxygen. They also grow taller and larger than other trees in wetlands. The roots of the tree help anchor it to the soil, so it does not get knocked over by the wind or floods. The roots also absorb water, so they prevent soil erosion.

B

1 The roots are known as knees since that is what they look like.
2 Plant scientists say vertical roots let the tree take in more oxygen than other trees.
3 Bald cypress trees living on dry land do not have roots above the soil.
4 The roots do not go into the soil because they are growing upward.
5 The vertical roots might make the horizontal ones more stable, but this needs to be researched more.

⊘ Summary

The bald cypress tree has aboveground roots called knees. Botanists say that the roots let the tree absorb more oxygen than other trees. But a comparison of trees growing in water and on dry land showed no significant difference in oxygen levels. In addition, the vertical roots growing above the ground do not anchor the tree in the soil. The horizontal roots growing in the soil do, however, anchor the tree.

Synthesizing

1 Although the author of the reading passage claims the tree can more easily absorb oxygen from the air, the professor states that is not precisely true.
2 Whereas the reading passage claims the trees are taller and larger because they take in more oxygen, the professor claims that a study showed wetland cypress trees did not have significantly higher levels of oxygen.
3 The reading passage mentions that the many roots let the tree anchor itself to the ground better, but the professor says that the roots growing above the soil do not go into the ground.
4 While the reading passage states that high winds and floods do not knock the tree over, the professor notes that the horizontal roots are the anchors.

Organization

1 The lecture and the reading passage both discuss the bald cypress tree.
2 However, the professor casts doubt on the points the author of the reading passage makes.
3 First, the professor covers the roots and the amount of oxygen they take in.
4 While the author of the reading passage declares that bald cypress tree roots take in more oxygen than the roots of other trees, the professor disagrees.
5 She mentions a comparison between cypresses growing on land and in the water.

6 According to her, <u>the ones growing in the water did not absorb much more oxygen.</u>

7 Second, the professor does not agree with <u>the comment in the reading passage that the aboveground roots of the bald cypress anchor it to the ground.</u>

8 She states that <u>the roots are vertical and do not go into the soil.</u>

9 Instead, horizontal roots <u>grow down into the soil and keep the tree in the ground.</u>

10 As a result, the professor <u>effectively counters the arguments made in the reading passage.</u>

Writing

Sample Response

The lecture and the reading passage both discuss the bald cypress tree. However, the professor casts doubt on the points the author of the reading passage makes.

First, the professor covers the roots and the amount of oxygen they take in. While the author of the reading passage declares that bald cypress tree roots take in more oxygen than the roots of other trees, the professor disagrees. She mentions a comparison between cypresses growing on land and in the water. According to her, the ones growing in the water did not absorb much more oxygen.

Second, the professor does not agree with the comment in the reading passage that the aboveground roots of the bald cypress anchor it to the ground. She states that the roots are vertical and do not go into the soil. Instead, horizontal roots grow down into the soil and keep the tree in the ground.

As a result, the professor effectively counters the arguments made in the reading passage.

해석

강의와 읽기 지문 모두 낙우송에 대해 논의하고 있다. 하지만 교수는 읽기 지문의 저자가 제기한 논점들에 의문을 제기한다.

첫째, 교수는 낙우송의 뿌리와 이들이 흡수하는 산소의 양을 언급한다. 낙우송의 뿌리가 다른 나무의 뿌리에 비해 더 많은 산소를 흡수한다고 읽기 지문의 저자는 주장하지만 교수는 이에 동의하지 않는다. 그녀는 지상에서 자라는 낙우송과 물에서 자라는 낙우송에 관한 비교 연구를 언급한다. 그녀에 의하면 물에서 자라는 낙우송이 훨씬 더 많은 산소를 흡수하지는 않았다.

둘째, 교수는 지상에 나와 있는 뿌리가 낙우송을 지면에 고정시킨다는 읽기 지문의 주장에 동의하지 않는다. 그녀는 이 뿌리들이 수직근이며 땅에 박혀 있지 않다고 주장한다. 대신 수평근이 자라서 땅속으로 들어가 이들이 나무를 땅에 고정시킨다.

따라서 교수는 읽기 지문에서 제기된 논점을 효과적으로 반박하고 있다.

Unit 07 Zoology II

Exercise p.62

Reading

해석

남부 거주 돌고래는 독특한 범고래 무리에 해당되는데, 그 개체수가 꾸준히 감소하고 있다. 해양 생물학자들은 약 70에서 80마리가 남아 있다고 생각한다. 이들과 관련된 주요 이슈는 먹이 부족과 관련된 것이다.

남부 거주 돌고래는 북아메리카 서쪽 해안 근처의 태평양에서 서식한다. 이들은 주요 먹이원으로 북태평양의 대형 연어에 의존하고 있다. 하지만 최근에 북태평양의 대형 언어의 수가 급감했다. 먹이의 부족으로 돌고래들은 쇠약해졌고 오염 물질들로 인해 병에 걸릴 가능성이 높아졌다. 돌고래의 지방층에는 PCB와 같은 오염 물질들이 축적되어 있다. 돌고래들은 연어를 먹지 못하는 경우 지방층에서 영양분을 추출한다. 그러면 PCB가 신체 내에 유입되어 암컷 돌고래들이 유산을 할 수 있다.

또한 이 돌고래들은 자신이 선호하는 사냥 지역에 있는 선박의 소음 때문에 스트레스를 받을 수 있다. 돌고래들은 레이더와 비슷한 반향 정위를 이용하여 먹이를 찾는다. 돌고래들은 소리를 내는데, 이 소리가 퍼져 물체와 부딪히면 그 소리가 다시 돌아오게 된다. 이러한 행동으로 돌고래들은 연어를 찾아서 먹이를 먹는다. 하지만 프로펠러의 소음 때문에 반향 정위가 제대로 작동을 하지 못할 수 있다. 그 결과 돌고래들이 먹이를 찾는데 어려움을 겪게 된다.

Note Taking

1) Chinook salmon
2) blubber
3) Stressed
4) echolocation

Listening

Script 🎧 01-08

M Professor: In the past few decades, the southern resident orca population has been steadily declining. Unfortunately, we really don't understand why this is happening. There are some theories, but each of them has problems.

For example, some experts claim orcas cannot find enough food in their traditional hunting grounds. This lack of food is then making them vulnerable to illnesses from pollutants in the water. It's an interesting theory, but there's a big problem with it. You see, uh, other species of orcas and whales reside in the same areas. And they appear to have no problems finding food. They also absorb the same pollutants yet have no problem producing offspring.

Another theory states that noise from the propellers of boats is causing southern resident orcas to fail to find enough food. Yet again, a comparison of other orcas and species of whales shows these animals are not affected. Scientists have also measured the noise levels created by boats. They have learned that the amount of noise is similar to that caused by storms in the ocean. There is no evidence that storm noise prevents orcas from finding food. As such, the search for the cause of their decline must continue.

해석

M Professor: 지난 수십 년 동안 남부 거주 돌고래의 개체수는 꾸준히 감소해 왔어요. 안타깝게도 우리는 왜 이런 일이 일어나고 있는지 사실 모르고 있습니다. 몇 가지 이론이 있기는 하지만 각각 문제를 가지고 있죠.

예를 들어 일부 전문가들은 돌고래들이 기존에 사냥하던 장소에서 충분한 음식을 찾지 못한다고 주장합니다. 이러한 먹이의 부족으로 그들이 수중 오염 물질에 의한 질병에 취약해지고 있다는 것이죠. 흥미로운 이론이지만 여기에는 커다란 문제가 있어요. 아시다시피, 어, 다른 돌고래 및 고래의 종들도 같은 지역에서 서식하고 있습니다. 그리고 이들은 전혀 먹이를 찾는데 문제를 겪고 있지 않은 것처럼 보입니다. 또한 동일한 오염 물질을 흡수하고 있지만 번식에 아무런 문제를 겪고 있지 않아요.

또 다른 이론은 선박의 프로펠러에서 나오는 소음 때문에 남부 거주 돌고래들이 충분한 먹이를 구하지 못한다고 주장합니다. 하지만 또 다시 다른 돌고래 및 고래종들과 비교를 해 보면 이들은 영향을 받고 있지 않아요. 과학자들은 또한 선박에서 나타나는 소음의 수준을 측정했습니다. 소음의 양이 바다에서 발생하는 폭풍우에 의한 소음과 비슷하다는 점을 알아냈죠. 폭풍우에 의한 소음으로 돌고래들이 먹이를 찾지 못한다는 증거는 존재하지 않습니다. 따라서 그 수가 감소하는 원인을 찾으려는 노력은 계속되어야 합니다.

✏️ **Note Taking**

1) orcas and whales
2) offspring
3) not affected
4) storms

Comparing the Points

Reasons for Orca Decline

Reading (Main Points)	Listening (Main Points)
Southern resident orcas' main food source, Chinook salmon, are disappearing, so the whales cannot find food. They have pollutants in their blubber, and when it gets released into their bodies, it causes miscarriages.	Other orcas and whales live in the same hunting grounds, but they can find food with no problems. They also absorb the same pollutants but can produce offspring.
Noise from boats disturbs the echolocation that orcas use to hunt. As a result, the orcas have trouble finding food.	Other orcas and whales are not affected by the propeller noise. It is as loud as a storm in the ocean, and orcas can usually find food during storms.

Paraphrasing & Summarizing

A

1 A group of killer whales called southern resident orcas are seeing their numbers go down.

2 Lately, the Chinook salmon population is dropping.

3 The PCBs get into their bodies and then make females lose their babies.

4 Orcas send out noises that reflect back to them from anything they hit.

5 But propeller noise makes orcas' radar have problems working.

✒️ **Summary**

Southern resident orcas are dealing with a declining population. They mostly eat Chinook salmon, but the number of salmon is plummeting. The orcas cannot get enough food. They also get pollutants like PCBs in their blubber. When PCBs get into their bodies, female orcas can have miscarriages. Orcas are also stressed by noise from boats' propellers. These cause their echolocation not to work properly, so they have trouble finding food.

B

1 For many years, the number of southern resident orcas has been going down.

2 For instance, some state that orcas cannot catch enough food where they hunt.

3 They are exposed to the same pollutants but still bear young.

4 Another thought is that propellers on boats are making too much noise for orcas to obtain food.

5 They know that the noise created is the same as the noise made by ocean storms.

✒️ **Summary**

In recent decades, the southern resident orca population has been declining. But there are some problems with the theories about why. Some experts say orcas cannot find enough food in their hunting grounds. But other orcas and whales can find food in the same places. They also have no problems producing offspring. Some also state that noise from boat propellers is disturbing orcas. But other orcas and whales are not affected.

Synthesizing

1 Even though the author of the reading passage writes that Chinook salmon numbers have plummeted, the professor comments that other orcas and whales can find food in the same places.

2 While the reading passage notes that PCBs can cause miscarriages in female orcas, the professor remarks that

other animals absorb the same pollutants yet can still produce offspring.

3   The reading passage claims that orcas can be stressed by boat noise in their hunting areas, yet the professor states that other orcas and whales are not affected.

4   Whereas the reading passage argues that propeller noise can cause problems for echolocation, the professor compares the noise level to that of an ocean storm.

Organization

1   The author of the reading passage discusses two reasons why southern resident orca numbers are declining.

2   However, the professor challenges these claims in his lecture.

3   The reading passage notes that orcas cannot get enough food in their traditional hunting grounds.

4   They are also taking in pollutants in their blubber, which can cause females to have miscarriages.

5   However, the professor points out that other orcas and whales in the same areas can find enough food.

6   He adds that these other creatures are not negatively affected by pollutants.

7   Next, the reading passage covers the noise made by boat propellers.

8   While the author of the reading passage states that the noise disrupts orca echolocation, the professor remarks that other orcas and whales are not affected.

9   He mentions that the noise made by propellers is the same as the noise made by storms.

10 Storms do not prevent orcas from hunting successfully.

11 The professor therefore shows some problems with the claims made in the reading passage.

Writing

Sample Response

The author of the reading passage discusses two reasons why southern resident orca numbers are declining. However, the professor challenges these claims in his lecture.

The reading passage notes that orcas cannot get enough food in their traditional hunting grounds. They are also taking in pollutants in their blubber, which can cause females to have miscarriages. However, the professor points out that other orcas and whales in the same areas can find enough food. He adds that these other creatures are not negatively affected by pollutants.

Next, the reading passage covers the noise made by boat propellers. While the author of the reading passage states that the noise disrupts orca echolocation, the professor remarks that other orcas and whales are not affected. He mentions that the noise made by propellers is the same as the noise made by storms. Storms do not prevent orcas from hunting successfully.

The professor therefore shows some problems with the claims made in the reading passage.

해석

읽기 지문의 저자는 남부 거주 돌고래들의 수가 감소하는 두 가지 이유에 대해 논의한다. 하지만 교수는 강의에서 그러한 주장을 반박하고 있다.

읽기 지문은 돌고래들이 기존의 사냥 지역에서 충분한 양의 먹이를 구할 수 없다는 점에 주목한다. 또한 지방층에는 오염 물질이 존재하는데, 이는 암컷들이 유산을 하는 원인이 될 수 있다. 하지만 같은 지역에 사는 다른 돌고래 및 고래들은 충분한 먹이를 찾을 수 있다는 점을 교수는 지적한다. 그는 덧붙여서 다른 생물들은 오염 물질로부터 부정적인 영향을 받고 있지 않다고 말한다.

다음으로 읽기 지문은 선박의 프로펠러에 의해 만들어지는 소음을 언급한다. 읽기 지문의 저자는 그러한 소음이 돌고래의 반향 정위를 방해한다고 주장하지만 교수는 다른 돌고래들과 고래들은 영향을 받지 않는다고 말한다. 그는 프로펠러의 소음이 폭풍우의 소음과 동일한 수준이라고 언급한다. 폭풍우는 돌고래의 성공적인 사냥을 막지 않는다.

따라서 교수는 읽기 지문에서 제기된 주장과 관련된 몇 가지 문제점을 보여준다.

Unit 08 Environmental Science

Exercise p.70

Reading

해석

많은 사람들이 다량의 의류를 구입하는 경향이 있는데, 이러한 의류는 시간이 지나도 거의 해어지지 않는다. 이러한 중고 의류들은 공간을 차지하기 때문에 사람들은 종종 이들 의류를 재활용할 것을 추천한다. 기부함이나 중고 의류를 취급하는 곳에 가지고 가면 된다. 하지만 중고 의류를 재활용하는 것은 사실 현명한 선택이 아니다.

우선 중고 의류를 재활용하기 위해서는 많은 비용이 요구된다. 의류 기부함은 보통 강판이나 고품질 플라스틱으로 만들어진다. 따라서 제작 비용이 비싸다. 또한 매일 서비스가 이루어져야 하기 때문에 내용물을 비우기 위해서는 누군가가 비용을 지불해야 한다. 또한 그 후에는 의류가 트럭으로 옮겨져서 재활용 센터로 보내져야 한다. 트럭, 연료, 그리고 운전자의 급여로 훨씬 더 많은 돈이 들어가게 된다.

두 번째 이슈는 중고 의류 재활용으로 생성되는 오염 물질과 관련이 있다. 재활용품 처리 공장으로 의류를 운반하는 트럭은 연료를 연소시킨다. 이로써 오염 물질이 대기에 유입된다. 재활용품 처리 공장 그 자체도 연료와 전기를 사용하며, 그 결과 더 많은 오염 물질이 생성된다. 마지막으로 기부된 의류 중 상당수는 재활용에 적합하지 않은 것이다. 따라서 이들은 결국 매립지로 보내지는데, 이로써 훨씬 더 많은 오염이 발생한다.

는 더 많은 에너지를 사용하여 새 옷을 만듭니다. 옷이 만들어지면 매장으로 운송되는데, 이때 훨씬 더 많은 오염이 발생해요.

✏ Note Taking

1) Clothing donation
2) trucks, fuel
3) recycling plants
4) unsuitable for recycling

✏ Note Taking

1) clothing retailers
2) wealth
3) pesticides
4) textile mills

Listening

Script 🎧 01-09

W Professor: In the United States alone, around eleven million tons of used clothes are generated each year. This is creating a serious issue regarding the recycling of these items. Critics of recycling used clothes claim it's too expensive and causes pollution. But I don't think they're actually correct.

Rather than sending undesired clothing to recycling plants, people can take it to used clothing retailers. There are many stores that accept clothing donations by people. The clothes are first mended and cleaned and then offered for sale at low prices. The money earned from these sales is often donated to charity or used to fund various social projects. So instead of costing money to recycle, used clothes can create wealth and improve people's lives.

Pollution is another issue associated with used clothing. Yet making new clothes to replace old ones creates even more pollution. For instance, cotton is a common clothing material. Farmers need pesticides and water to grow cotton. The cotton must then be transported to textile mills, where more energy is used to make new clothes. Once the clothes are made, they are transported to stores, which creates even more pollution.

해석

W Professor: 미국에서만 약 1,100만 톤의 중고 의류가 매년 배출되고 있어요. 이로 인해 이들 제품의 재활용과 관련된 중대한 이슈가 제기되고 있습니다. 중고 의류의 재활용을 비판하는 사람들은 그 비용이 너무 높고 그로 인해 오염이 발생한다고 주장을 하죠. 하지만 저는 그들의 말이 실제로 옳다고 생각하지 않습니다.

원치 않는 의류를 재활용품 처리 공장으로 보내는 대신 사람들은 이를 중고 의류 판매점으로 가지고 갈 수 있어요. 의류를 기부할 수 있는 많은 매장들이 존재합니다. 먼저 의류를 수선하고 세탁한 후에 낮은 가격으로 의류를 판매하죠. 이러한 판매로 거두어들인 수익은 종종 자선 단체에 기부되거나 다양한 사회 사업을 후원하는데 사용됩니다. 따라서 중고 의류는, 비용을 들여 재활용을 할 필요없이, 부를 창출하고 사람들의 삶을 향상시킬 수 있습니다.

중고 의류와 관련된 또 다른 문제는 오염이에요. 하지만 기존 의류를 대체하기 위해 새 의류를 만드는 것이 훨씬 더 많은 오염을 발생시킵니다. 예를 들어 면은 일반적으로 사용되는 의류 소재예요. 농부들이 면을 재배하기 위해서는 살충제와 물이 필요하죠. 그런 다음 면은 방직 공장으로 운송되어야 하며, 그곳에서

Comparing the Points

Recycling Used Clothing

Reading (Main Points)	Listening (Main Points)
There are expenses such as clothing donation boxes and paying people who serve them when it comes to recycling used clothing. Transporting them to recycling centers costs even more money.	People can donate used clothing to retailers, who sell it for low prices. The money is donated to charity or used for social projects, so wealth is created, and people's lives are improved.
Recycling used clothing also creates pollution, such as by trucks and recycling plants. In addition, donated clothing is sometimes unsuitable, so it goes to landfills, which makes more pollution.	Making new clothes creates more pollution than recycling used clothes. Growing cotton, transporting it to textile mills, and then sending clothes to stores all create lots of pollution.

Paraphrasing & Summarizing

A

1 Many people buy lots of clothing but almost never wear it.
2 Boxes used clothes are put in are built with steel or plastic.
3 It costs more money for trucks, fuel, and drivers' wages.
4 The recycling center makes more pollution from the fuel and electricity it uses.
5 A lot of donated clothes cannot be recycled.

✐ Summary

Lots of people donate their used clothing, but that is not always a smart thing to do. Among the expenses of donating clothing are the donation boxes and the salaries of those servicing them. Transporting the clothes to recycling centers requires additional payments. Recycling used clothes creates pollution, too. The trucks and the recycling plants use fuel that makes pollution. And many clothes cannot be recycled, so they go to landfills, which makes even more pollution.

B

1 Americans produce around eleven million tons of used clothes annually.

2 Instead of recycling used clothes, people can give them to used clothing stores.

3 Profits from sales may be given to charity or used to pay for social projects.

4 But more pollution is made when people produce new clothes.

5 After making clothes, they are taken to stores, which makes more pollution.

✏ Summary

It is not right to say that recycling used clothes is expensive and causes pollution. First, people can donate used clothes to stores that sell them. Then, the money is often donated to charity or used for social projects. So recycling used clothes can create wealth and help others. Next, making new clothes produces more pollution than recycling old clothes. The costs include growing cotton and transporting it and then taking clothes to stores.

Synthesizing

1 The author of the reading passage describes the cost of making clothing donations boxes, so the professor suggests that people take used clothes to clothing retailers.

2 While the reading passage mentions some costs involved, the professor says that money from sales of used clothes goes to charity or fund social projects.

3 Although the reading passage states that recycling plants produce pollution, the professor points out what is needed to grow cotton.

4 Whereas the reading passage states that clothing in landfills creates pollution, the professor remarks that taking it to stores make more pollution.

Organization

1 Both the lecture and the reading passage focus on the issue of recycling used clothing.

2 In her talk, the professor challenges the two arguments made in the reading passage.

3 While the reading passage describes how expensive recycling clothes is, the professor says that people can donate clothes to used clothing retailers.

4 Then, these stores will sell the clothes.

5 The money is often donated to good causes, so many people can benefit from these clothing donations.

6 Next, the professor refutes the argument made about pollution creation in the reading passage.

7 The author claims that the process of donating clothes creates a large amount of pollution.

8 But the professor counters that argument by stating that the act of making new clothes creates even more pollution.

9 For instance, growing cotton to make clothes and then transporting the clothes produces a large amount of pollution.

10 By focusing on these two arguments, the professor challenges the ones made in the reading passage.

Writing

Sample Response

Both the lecture and the reading passage focus on the issue of recycling used clothing. In her talk, the professor challenges the two arguments made in the reading passage.

While the reading passage describes how expensive recycling clothes is, the professor says that people can donate clothes to used clothing retailers. Then, these stores will sell the clothes. The money is often donated to good causes, so many people can benefit from these clothing donations.

Next, the professor refutes the argument made about pollution creation in the reading passage. The author claims that the process of recycling clothes creates a large amount of pollution. But the professor counters that argument by stating that the act of making new clothes creates even more pollution. For instance, growing cotton to make clothes and then transporting the clothes produces a large amount of pollution.

By focusing on these two arguments, the professor challenges the ones made in the reading passage.

해석

강의와 읽기 지문 모두 중고 의류 재활용에 관한 이슈에 초점을 맞추고 있다. 강의에서 교수는 읽기 지문에서 제기된 두 가지 논점을 반박한다.

읽기 지문은 의류 재활용에 막대한 비용이 든다고 설명하지만 교수는 사람들이 의류를 중고 의류 매장에 기부할 수 있다고 말한다. 그러면 이들 매장에서 의류가 판매될 것이다. 그로 인한 수익은 종종 자선 단체에 기부되기 때문에 많은 사람들이 이러한 의류 기부로 혜택을 받을 수 있다.

다음으로 교수는 오염 발생에 관한 읽기 지문의 주장을 반박한다. 작가는 의류를 재활용하는 과정에서 다량의 오염 물질이 발생한다고 주장한다. 하지만 교수는 새로운 의류를 만드는 행위로 훨씬 더 많은 오염이 발생한다고 언급함으로써 그러한 주장을 반박한다. 예를 들어 옷을 만들기 위해 면을 재배하고 옷을 운반하는 과정에서 다량의 오염 물질이 배출된다.

이러한 두 가지 논점에 초점을 맞추면서 교수는 읽기 지문에서 제기된 논점들에 이의를 제기한다.

Unit 09 Environmental Science

Exercise 1 .... p.84

Brainstorming & Outlining

A

Professor Jarvis

해석

오늘날 환경은 열악한 상태에 놓여 있습니다. 토지, 대기, 그리고 수질과 관련된 문제들이 있죠. 많은 기업들이, 특히 공장들이, 오염 물질을 발생시킵니다. 기업들이 환경을 보호하기 위해 더 많은 노력을 해야 한다고 생각하나요? 아니면 그들이 아무것도 할 필요가 없을까요? 왜 그런가요?

B

Russell

해석

기업들은 분명 환경을 보호하기 위해 더 많은 노력을 해야 합니다. 어쨌거나 기업이 오염을 일으키고 있으니까요. 기업들은 전 세계에서 문제를 일으키고 있습니다. 그들은 자신이 만든 오물들을 치우기 위한 자금을 제공해야 해요. 그리고 그처럼 많은 오염 물질을 더 이상 배출해서는 안 될 것입니다.

🖉 Summary Notes: Russell

1) polluting environment
2) more
3) around the world
4) funds
5) messes
6) creating

Martina

해석

저는 기업들이 자신이 초래한 오염에 대해 아무것도 할 필요가 없다고 생각합니다. 어쨌거나 그들이 따라야 하는 법이 정부에 존재하니까요. 정부는 분명 어느 정도의 오염 물질 배출은 용인할 수 있다고 생각합니다. 기업들은 그러한 법을 준수하고 있기 때문에 별다른 조치를 취할 필요가 없습니다.

🖉 Summary Notes: Martina

1) do anything
2) regulations
3) follow
4) some pollution
5) obeying law
6) need

Organization
Supporting Russell's Opinion

1   While I understand Martina's argument, I believe businesses must act to protect the environment.

2   As Russell points out, businesses are causing environmental problems.

3   In my city, one factory is polluting a local lake.

4   It should be responsible for cleaning the lake and purifying the water.

5   In addition, businesses are major polluters.

6   They pollute much more than individuals.

7   If they clean up pollution and then produce less of it, the world will be a better place to live.

8   Businesses therefore must act and fix the problems they make.

Supporting Martina's Opinion

1   I agree with Martina and do not think businesses are responsible for cleaning up pollution.

2   Martina is correct that as long as businesses obey the law, they should not have to do anything else.

3   The government could, of course, change the law.

4   But that is not the responsibility of businesses.

5   Another point is that overall, individuals pollute the world much more than businesses.

6   So many people litter everywhere.

7   They create huge amounts of trash.

8   Individuals are polluting the world.

9   We should not accuse businesses of harming the environment.

Exercise 2 .... p.87

Professor Merriweather

해석

목요일 수업에서는 재활용 과정에 대해 논의할 거예요. 최근 몇십 년 동안 재활용이 흔해졌습니다. 많은 정부들이 재활용을 요구하며 장려하고 있죠. 하지만 모든 사람들이 이를 지지하는 것은 아닙니다. 사람들이 재활용을 더 많이 해야 한다고 생각하나요? 아니면 재활용이 실제로는 환경에 도움이 되지 않을까요? 그 이유는요?

Emily

해석

재활용은 환경에 매우 도움이 됩니다. 사람들은 반드시 재활용을 더 많이 해야 해요. 과학 기술의 발전 덕분에 우리는 온갖 종류의 물품들을 재활용할 수 있습니다. 이로써 천연 자원에 대한 의존도를 낮추고 미래 세대를 위해 자원을 비축할 수 있습니다.

Robert

해석

대부분의 물건을 재활용할 필요는 없습니다. 예를 들어 나무는 재생이 가능한 자원이기 때문에 종이는 재활용을 할 필요가 없어요. 유리는 규소로 만들어집니다. 이는 지구 전체에서 풍부하게 존재하는 것이죠. 현재 하고 있는 것 정도로 재활용을 할 필요는 없습니다.

Sample Response 1 Supporting Emily

Robert makes a good point, yet Emily makes a better one. There are many resources that we should recycle these days. For instance, silver is used in numerous electronic appliances. There is a limited amount of it on the Earth. However, people do not recycle phones and laptops but just throw them away. People should definitely recycle those items. We should also recycle plastic items instead of throwing them away. Plastic fills up landfills. By recycling it, we can keep the Earth clean. For those two reasons, I think we should recycle more.

해석

Robert가 좋은 지적을 했지만 Emily의 지적이 더 훌륭하다. 오늘날 우리가 재활용해야 하는 많은 자원들이 존재한다. 예를 들어 은은 여러 전자 기기에서 사용된다. 지구상의 은의 양은 제한되어 있다. 하지만 사람들은 전화기 및 노트북을 재활용하지 않고 그냥 폐기해 버린다. 사람들은 반드시 이러한 제품들을 재활용해야 한다. 또한 플라스틱 제품들도 폐기하는 대신 재활용을 해야 한다. 플라스틱이 매립지를 채우고 있다. 이를 재활용함으로써 우리는 지구를 깨끗하게 만들 수 있다. 이러한 두 가지 이유에서 나는 재활용을 더 많이 해야 한다고 생각한다.

Sample Response 2 Supporting Robert

I fully agree with Robert that it is not necessary to recycle. Paper and glass products come from renewable resources. We can get as many of those resources as we want. Recycling paper and glass is a waste of time and money. In addition, many items that people send to recycling centers do not actually get recycled. Instead, they are simply crushed and sent to garbage dumps. This is an enormous waste of people's time and money. People are just recycling for no reason. So they should stop doing it.

해석

나는 재활용이 필요하지 않다는 Robert의 입장에 전적으로 동의한다. 종이 및 유리 제품은 재생이 가능한 자원으로 만들어진다. 우리는 원하는 만큼 이들 자원을 많이 구할 수 있다. 종이와 유리를 재활용하는 것은 시간 낭비이자 돈 낭비이다. 게다가 사람들이 재활용품 처리장으로 보내는 많은 제품들이 실제로는 재활용되지 않는다. 그 대신 분쇄되어 쓰레기 처리장으로 보내진다. 이는 막대한 시간 낭비이자 돈 낭비이다. 사람들은 아무런 이유 없이 재활용을 하고 있다. 따라서 이를 중단해야 한다.

Unit 10 Education I

Exercise 1 .... p.90

Brainstorming & Outlining

A

Professor Cartwright

해석

고등학교 교과 과정에 대해 논의해 보죠. 대부분의 학교들이 수학, 과학, 그리고 역사와 같은 학문에 집중하고 있습니다. 하지만 요리, 청소, 그리고 개인 자산 관리와 같은 기본적인 생활 스킬을 가르치는 곳도 있어요. 모든 고등학교가 기본적인 생활 스킬을 가르쳐야 한다고 생각하나요, 아니면 학문만 가르쳐야 한다고 생각하나요? 그 이유는요?

B

Sandra

해석

저는 고등학교에서 기본적인 생활 스킬을 가르치면 좋겠어요. 너무나 많은 학생들이 책에 있는 내용만 배우고 실용적인 지식은 결여한 상태로 졸업을 합니다. 고등학교들은 학생들의 졸업 이후의 삶에도 도움이 될 수 있도록 가정 경제 수업을 가르치기 시작해야 해요.

✍ Summary Notes: Sandra

1) basic life skills
2) book knowledge
3) practical knowledge
4) home economics
5) after graduation

Wilson

해석

학교의 목적은 학문을 가르치는 것이어야 합니다. 학생들은 고등학교에서 수학, 과학, 역사, 그리고 기타 유사한 과목들에 관한 지식을 배우고 있죠. 기본적인 생활 스킬에 대해 말하자면, 이는 학부모들이 책임져야 하는 것입니다. 학교가 여기에 관심을 기울여서는 안 됩니다.

✍ Summary Notes: Wilson

1) academic subjects
2) math, science
3) responsibility
4) concerned

Organization
Supporting Sandra's Opinion

1 Sandra is correct in stating that high schools should teach students basic life skills.

2 My older sister had a difficult time after graduating from high school.

3 She lived alone but could not cook, clean, or do other similar activities.

Answers, Scripts, and Translations **21**

4 It took her a long time to learn and gave her a lot of stress.

5 In addition, high schools should focus on all aspects of learning.

6 Academics are important but not the only thing.

7 That is why schools also have sports teams.

8 Adding classes in basic life skills will help make well-adjusted students ready for life as adults.

Supporting Wilson's Opinion

1 I like the way that Wilson thinks.

2 High school students should learn math and science, not cooking.

3 Teaching basic life skills is for parents.

4 My parents taught me to cook and clean.

5 I know other parents can do the same thing for their children.

6 In addition, high schools should prepare students for college.

7 Colleges do not care if students can cook or clean.

8 They only care about the knowledge students have.

9 High schools should therefore not waste time on unimportant subjects.

10 The only topics high schools should teach are academic ones.

Exercise 2 ·· p.93

Professor Holmes
해석

요즘 대학 등록금이 믿을 수 없을 정도로 높습니다. 많은 학생들이 등록금을 낼 형편이 되지 못해서 대출을 받고 있죠. 안타깝게도 많은 학생들이 현재 막대한 빚을 지고 있습니다. 한 가지 아이디어를 소개할게요. 정부가 모든 학자금 대출을 무효화해야 한다. 여기에 찬성하나요, 아니면 반대하나요? 그 이유는요?

Ernest
해석

저는 정부가 모든 학자금 대출을 무효화시켜야 한다는데 동의합니다. 대학에 다니면 터무니 없이 많은 돈이 들어요. 하지만 사람들은 취직을 하기 위해 대학에 다녀야만 하죠. 젊은 사람들이 그처럼 많은 빚을 지는 것은 공정하지 않습니다. 많은 사람들이 대출금을 결코 갚지 못할 것이기 때문에 대출은 무효화되어야 해요.

Sally
해석

저는 그러한 주장을 강력히 반대합니다. 대출을 받은 학생들은 대출금을 갚아야 해요. 그것이 올바른 일이죠. 정부가 자동차 대출이나 주택 담보 대출을 이용한 사람들의 부채를 무효화시키지는 않습니다. 따라서 학자금 대출에 있어서도 그럴 이유가 전혀 없어요.

Sample Response 1 Supporting Ernest

> I understand the point that Sally makes, but Ernest is correct. The government really should cancel all student

> debt. People have to attend college to get good jobs, but college is too expensive these days. Making poor students pay back loans they were forced to take is wrong. In addition, so many young people have tens of thousands of dollars in debt. Because of their debt, they cannot get married, have children, or buy houses. They have sad futures ahead of them unless the government cancels their debt.

해석

나는 Sally의 논점을 이해하지만 Ernest의 말이 옳다. 정부가 실제로 모든 학자금 대출을 무효화해야 한다. 사람들은 좋은 직장을 구하기 위해 대학에 다녀야 하지만 요즘 대학 등록금이 너무나 비싸다. 어쩔 수 없이 받은 대출금을 가난한 학생들에게 갚도록 하는 것은 잘못된 일이다. 또한 너무나 많은 젊은 사람들이 수만 달러의 빚을 지고 있다. 빚 때문에 결혼도 할 수 없고, 아이도 가질 수 없으며, 집을 살 수도 없다. 정부가 빚을 무효화하지 않는 이상 그들의 앞에는 불행한 미래만 있을 뿐이다.

Sample Response 2 Supporting Sally

> I cannot agree with Ernest because there is no reason for the government to cancel student loans. As Sally notes, people must repay loans for cars and homes. They should also repay student loans. After all, nobody forced them to take out those loans. While it is true that students should attend college to get good jobs, they can still go to inexpensive schools. Many schools have cheap tuition but provide good educations. Students need to take responsibility for their actions and pay back their loans.

해석

정부가 학자금 대출을 무효화시킬 아무런 이유도 없기 때문에 나는 Ernest의 의견에 동의할 수 없다. Sally가 지적한 대로 사람들은 자동차나 주택을 담보로 받은 대출금을 갚아야 한다. 학자금 대출 또한 갚아야 하는 것이다. 어찌되었든 그들이 대출을 받도록 강요한 사람은 없었다. 학생들이 좋은 직장을 구하기 위해 대학을 다녀야 한다는 점은 사실이지만, 그러면 비싸지 않은 학교에 다니면 된다. 등록금이 저렴한 많은 학교들도 양질의 교육을 제공한다. 학생들은 자신의 행동에 대한 책임을 져야 하며 자신의 대출금을 갚아야 한다.

Unit 11 Sociology I

Exercise 1 ·· p.96

Brainstorming & Outlining

A

Professor Lamplighter
해석

이제 여러분들이 여가 활동 및 레저 활동에 대해 생각해 보면 좋을 것 같군요. 여가 시간이 있는 경우에 사람들은 여러 가지 다양한 활동을 하게 됩니다. 여러분은 여가 활동을 혼자서 하는 것을 선호하나요? 아니면 다른 사람들과 같이 하는 것을 선호하나요? 그 이유는요?

B

Calvin

해석

제 취미는 모두 저 혼자서 하는 것이기 때문에 저는 혼자서 하는 것을 선호합니다. 저는 여가 시간에 풍경화와 정물화를 그립니다. 또한 때때로 비행기와 선박을 대상으로 삼기도 하죠. 이러한 것들은 다른 사람과 함께 할 수 있는 활동이 아니에요.

✏️ Summary Notes: Calvin

1) painting
2) landscapes
3) still lifes
4) models
5) airplanes
6) ships

Shannon

해석

저는 레저 활동을 할 때 항상 누군가와 같이 해요. 예를 들어 저는 인근의 국립 공원에서 등산하는 것을 좋아합니다. 이러한 활동은 종종 제 오빠랑 하고 있어요. 저의 또 다른 여가 활동은 영화를 보는 것입니다. 저는 친한 친구들과 주말마다 함께 영화를 보러 가는 경우가 많아요.

✏️ Summary Notes: Shannon

1) hiking
2) brother
3) movies
4) close friends
5) weekends

Organization

Supporting Calvin's Opinion

1 Calvin and I have a lot in common because we both prefer doing hobbies alone.
2 While he enjoys painting pictures, I prefer to draw pictures.
3 I often draw pictures of people and animals.
4 For me, this hobby is quite relaxing.
5 Another hobby of mine is playing the piano.
6 We have a piano at my home, and I love to play different songs on it.
7 I mostly play pop songs, but I also know some classical music.
8 These two hobbies are ones that I do all by myself.

Supporting Shannon's Opinion

1 While I understand why Calvin does hobbies alone, my style is more like Shannon's.

2 However, I do not do the hobbies that she does.
3 One of my hobbies is playing basketball.
4 My best friend and I often play basketball in the evenings and on weekends.
5 We have lots of fun together.
6 Another one of my hobbies is cooking.
7 My mother and I bake bread and cookies when we have free time.
8 It is such a fun activity, and I love spending time with my mother.
9 These hobbies that I do with others are great.

Exercise 2 ·· p.99

Professor Benjamin

해석

오늘날 소셜 미디어가 많은 사람들, 특히 젊은 사람들에게 막대한 인기를 얻고 있습니다. 소셜 미디어에는 많은 인플루언서들이 존재해요. 이 사람들은 수천 혹은 수백만 명의 팔로워들을 보유하고 있는데, 이들은 그들이 하는 말에 큰 주의를 기울입니다. 소셜 미디어의 인플루언서들이 사람들에게 긍정적인 영향을 끼친다고 생각하나요, 아니면 부정적인 영향을 끼친다고 생각하나요? 그 이유는요?

Ronald

해석

전체적으로 저는 소셜 미디어의 인플루언서들이 팔로워들에게 긍정적인 영향을 미친다고 말하고 싶습니다. 저는 몇몇 인플루언서들의 팟캐스트를 시청하고 있어요. 그들은 자신의 팔로워들에게 영양가가 높은 음식을 먹고, 부모의 말에 신경을 쓰며, 착하게 행동하라고 말을 합니다. 제 생각으로는 그들의 충고가 다른 사람들에게 긍정적인 영향을 미치는 것 같아요.

Christina

해석

대부분의 소셜 미디어 인플루언서들은 형편없는 사람들로서, 아무도 그들의 말에 귀를 기울여서는 안 됩니다. 너무나 많은 인플루언서들이 좋지 않은 이유로 유명해지고 있어요. 이러한 사람들은 종종 부도덕한 행동을 나타내며, 많은 사람들, 특히 십대들의 삶에 부정적인 영향을 미치고 있습니다.

Sample Response 1 **Supporting Ronald**

> I believe Christina is a bit too harsh. As for me, I side with Ronald. Ronald is right in that many social media influencers pass on positive messages to their followers. They encourage children and teens to be good people and to behave right. Something else they do is inspire people to be adventurous. Some influencers travel around the world. They do various activities in different countries. They show their followers how to have fun lives while doing exciting activities. These kinds of influencers are definitely positive.

해석

나는 Christina가 다소 냉혹한 편이라고 생각한다. 나로서는 Ronald와 입장이 같다. 많은 소셜 미디어 인플루언서들이 팔로워들에게 긍정적인 메시지를 전하고 있다는 Ronald의 말이 옳다. 그들은 아이들과 십대들에게 착한 사람이 되고 올바른 행동을 하라고 권유한다. 그 밖에도 사람들이 모험심을 갖도록 고무시킨다. 일부 인플루언서들은 전 세계를 여행한다. 그들은 다양한 국가에서 여러 가지 활동을 한다. 그들은 흥미진진한 활동을 하면서 팔로워들에게 어떻게 즐거운 삶을 살 수 있는지 보여 준다. 이러한 유형의 인플루언서들은 분명 긍정적이다.

Sample Response 2 Supporting Christina

> As far as I am aware, most social media influencers are negative role models. Christina is right regarding how many of them act. Recently, there have been some news reports about influencers who were arrested. They did a variety of illegal activities. Some influencers also use lots of bad language. They need to remember that children watch their podcasts. These children might try to imitate them and use bad language, too. To me, this makes them negative role models.

해석

내가 아는 한 대부분의 소셜 미디어 인플루언서들은 부정적인 롤 모델이다. 그들 중 많은 이들의 행동과 관련해서는 Christina의 말이 옳다. 체포된 인플루언서들에 관한 뉴스 보도가 최근에 이루어졌다. 그들은 여러 가지 불법적인 행동을 했다. 또한 몇몇 인플루언서들은 나쁜 말을 많이 사용한다. 그들은 어린이들도 자신의 팟캐스트를 보고 있다는 점을 기억해야 한다. 그러한 어린이들은 그들을 모방해서 마찬가지로 나쁜 말을 사용할 수도 있다. 내게는 이러한 점 때문에 그들이 부정적인 롤 모델로 보인다.

Unit 12 Education II

Exercise 1 .... p.102

Brainstorming & Outlining

A

Professor Arbuckle

해석

다음 수업 시간에는 방과후 활동에 대해 논의할 거예요. 토론 게시판의 주제를 알려 드리죠. 많은 학생들이 수업이 끝난 후 과외 활동에 참여하고 있습니다. 여러분은 방과후에 스포츠 활동을 하는 것을 선호하나요, 아니면 동아리 활동을 하는 것을 선호하나요? 그 이유는요?

B

Ryan

해석

저는 제가 운동을 잘 한다고 생각하기 때문에 방과후에 스포츠를 하고 싶습니다. 저는 농구와 축구와 같은 팀 스포츠를 좋아해요. 또한 테니스를 하는 것도 좋아하고요. 이러한 활동들은 재미있을 뿐만 아니라 좋은 운동이 됩니다. 게다가 저는 팀에 소속되는 것도 좋아해요.

Summary Notes: Ryan

1) athlete
2) basketball
3) soccer
4) team

Candice

해석

두 가지 중에서 선택을 해야 한다면 저는 동아리 활동을 택할 거예요. 많은 동아리들이 기본적으로 학문과 관련이 있습니다. 여기에는 수학과 과학 동아리가 포함되죠. 여기에 가입함으로써 저는 많은 것을 배울 수 있을 거예요. 다른 동아리들, 예컨대 체스 동아리와 사진 동아리는 취미를 위한 것들입니다. 마찬가지로 여기에 가입해도 재미있을 거예요.

Summary Notes: Candice

1) Academic
2) science
3) learn
4) Chess and photography
5) hobbies
6) join

Organization

Supporting Ryan's Opinion

1 While the clubs Candice describes sound interesting, I would prefer to play sports after school.
2 Ryan is correct in noting that sports are fun and great exercise.
3 When I play sports with my friends, we always have a great time.
4 I also find that I get in great shape.
5 Another positive factor about sports is winning games.
6 It feels great to be on a team that wins a game.
7 There really is nothing better than contributing to your team's victory.
8 For those reasons, I would play sports.

Supporting Candice's Opinion

1 I am like Candice and would rather do club activities than play sports.
2 Clubs that are for hobbyists are really fun.
3 I would like to join a computer programming club as well as a writing club.
4 In those clubs, I could improve my skills and become more talented.
5 If I also joined an academic club, I could learn more about a subject.
6 That would help me improve my grade in that subject while also increasing my knowledge.
7 Those reasons are important enough to make me want to do club activities.

Professor Vernon

해석

연구 조사를 통해 어린이와 십대들이 밤에 충분한 수면을 취하지 못하고 있다는 점이 입증되었습니다. 하지만 어린이와 십대들은 보통 일찍 일어나서 학교에 가야만 하죠. 학생들이 잠을 더 잘 수 있도록 학교가 평소보다 한 시간 늦게 수업을 시작해서 해야 한다고 생각하나요? 그 이유는요?

Andrew

해석

저는 그것이 훌륭한 아이디어라고 생각합니다. 저는 매일 아침 6시쯤에 일어나서 학교에 가야만 해요. 이는 너무 이른 시간으로, 저는 보통 자정에 잠자리에 듭니다. 학교가 더 늦은 시간에 수업을 시작한다면 제가 항상 그처럼 피곤해 하지는 않을 거예요.

Melanie

해석

매력적인 아이디어이긴 한데 저는 학교가 그렇게 해야 한다고 생각하지 않습니다. 대부분의 성인들도 학생들이 등교하는 시간과 같은 시간에 출근을 해요. 학교 수업이 한 시간 늦게 시작된다면 부모들이 자녀들을 학교에 데려다 줄 수 없을 것입니다.

Sample Response 1 Supporting Andrew

While Melanie makes a good argument, I agree with Andrew. Schools should start one hour later every day. As Andrew mentions, students would not be so tired because they would get more sleep. That would improve their performance at school. Another point is that by starting school later, students could avoid rush-hour traffic. They would no longer get stuck in traffic jams, so they would get to school faster. This means they would have even more time to sleep. Schools should change their starting times at once.

해석

Melanie의 주장에도 일리가 있지만 나는 Andrew의 의견에 동의한다. 학교는 매일 한 시간 늦게 수업을 시작해야 한다. Andrew가 언급한 것처럼 학생들은 잠을 더 많이 자게 되기 때문에 크게 피곤해 하지 않을 것이다. 그러면 학교 성적도 향상될 것이다. 또 다른 요점은 학교 수업을 늦게 시작함으로써 학생들이 출퇴근 시간대의 교통 체증을 피할 수 있다는 것이다. 더 이상 극심한 교통 체증에 시달릴 필요가 없으므로 학교에 더 빨리 도착하게 될 것이다. 이는 그들에게 잠을 잘 수 있는 시간이 더욱 늘어날 것이라는 점을 의미한다. 학교는 당장 수업 시작 시간을 바꾸어야 한다.

Sample Response 2 Supporting Melanie

Although I would love to start school later, I do not think that is possible. Melanie is right in pointing out that parents who work could not drop their children off at school. This would result in it being hard for many students to get to school. Something else to consider is that schools would have to finish later in the day. This would give students less time to do various activities after school. In winter, students in

many places would finish school when it is dark. I therefore believe schools should not change their starting times.

해석

나도 학교 수업이 더 늦게 시작하는 것을 바라지만 그런 일은 가능하지 않다고 생각한다. 일을 하는 부모들이 자녀들을 학교에 데려다 줄 수 없게 될 것이라는 Melanie의 지적은 옳다. 그 결과 많은 학생들이 통학하기가 힘들어질 것이다. 고려해야 할 또 다른 점은 학교 수업이 더 늦게 끝나게 될 것이라는 점이다. 이로써 학생들에게는 다양한 방과후 활동을 할 시간이 적어지게 될 것이다. 겨울에는 많은 지역의 학생들이 어두워질 때 학교 수업을 마치게 될 것이다. 따라서 나는 학교가 수업 시작 시간을 변경해서는 안 된다고 생각한다.

Unit 13 Economics

Exercise 1 ··· p.108

Brainstorming & Outlining

A

Professor Redwood

해석

다음 주 월요일에는 광고에 대해 논의할 거예요. 자, 다음에 대한 여러분들의 생각을 알고 싶군요. 대부분의 기업들은 자사의 제품 및 서비스를 광고합니다. 하지만 많은 광고들이 오해를 불러 일으키고 있어요. 잘못된 주장을 하거나 제품이 실제와 다르게 보이도록 만들죠. 오해의 소지가 있는 광고를 금지해야 할까요? 그 이유는요?

B

Kristine

해석

저는 오해의 소지가 있는 광고를 강력히 반대해요. 기업들이 그러한 광고를 이용하도록 허락해서는 안 됩니다. 저는 몇 차례 광고를 보고 제품을 구매했어요. 하지만 제품을 받았을 때 제품이 광고의 사진과 똑같지 않았죠. 그런 일은 잘못된 것이었고 허용되어서는 안 됩니다.

✏ Summary Notes: Kristine

1) misleading ads
2) Companies
3) ads
4) resemble pics
5) permitted

Edward

해석

오해의 소지가 있는 광고에 문제가 될 것은 없어요. 소비자들은 항상 광고를 경계해야 합니다. 광고가 사실을 왜곡하고 제품의 부정적인 측면은 전혀 보여 주지 않는다는 점은 모든 사람이 알고 있어요. 하지만 사람들은 여전히 광고에 속습니다. 이는 기업의 문제가 아니라 사람들의 문제인 것이에요.

Summary Notes: Edward

1) Nothing wrong
2) Consumers
3) bend the truth
4) negative
5) get fooled

Organization

Supporting Kristine's Opinion

1 I understand the point that Edward makes, but I disagree with him.
2 Kristine is correct in stating that misleading advertisements should be banned.
3 I too have been tricked by ads at times.
4 As a result, I have lost a lot of money.
5 I do not appreciate that.
6 In addition, children are very easy to trick with advertisements.
7 They are not sophisticated enough to understand that ads are not always honest.
8 It simply is not fair to allow ads that can easily separate children from their money.
9 Misleading ads should no longer be allowed.

Supporting Edward's Opinion

1 While it is unfortunate that people get tricked by ads, these ads should not be banned.
2 First, we should remember the phrase "Let the buyer beware."
3 This means that, like Edward notes, consumers should be cautious.
4 They should not believe everything a company claims about its products.
5 Second, people have the freedom to say anything they want in this country.
6 Even lying is permitted.
7 So if companies lie in their ads, that is fine.
8 When enough people learn a company lies, they will boycott the company.
9 Then, it will go bankrupt.
10 That is what we should do about misleading ads.

Exercise 2 .... p.111

Professor Nash

해석
중소기업은 우리 나라 경제에 중요합니다. 중소기업에는 종종 두세 명의 소유주가 존재해요. 많은 경우, 소유주들은 친구 사이입니다. 친구들은 함께 일을 잘 할 수도 있지만, 또한 심각한 문제에 직면할 수도 있어요. 사람들이 친구와 사업을 해야 한다고 생각하나요? 그 이유는요?

Isabella

해석
저는 친구들이 함께 사업을 해야 한다고 생각합니다. 우정 때문에 부지런히 일해서 사업을 성공시키려고 할 거예요. 많은 공동 소유주들이 서로 사이가 좋지 못합니다. 하지만 같이 사업을 하는 친구들은 최선을 다해 자신들의 문제를 해결하려고 할 거예요.

Bernard

해석
친구들이 함께 사업을 해야 한다는 것은 어리석은 생각입니다. 회사가 성공하지 못하거나 파산하는 경우, 정말 많은 이들의 우정이 갈라져요. 그런 일이 발생하면 사업과 우정 모두 영원히 사라지게 되죠.

Sample Response 1 Supporting Isabella

Isabella is correct in noting that friends can go into business together. My father and his best friend started a restaurant together. They have problems sometimes, but they always talk about them. Then, they solve their problems. The reason is their friendship. Another important factor is that my father and his friend know each other's personality. So they know what actions to do and what actions not to do. This helps them avoid arguments and get along great most of the time. Because they are friends, their restaurant is successful.

해석
친구들끼리 사업을 해도 된다는 Isabella의 주장이 옳다. 내 아버지와 아버지의 가장 친한 친구분은 함께 식당을 여셨다. 때때로 문제를 겪으시지만 항상 그에 대해 대화를 나누신다. 그러면 문제가 해결된다. 그 이유는 우정 때문이다. 또 다른 중요한 요인은 아버지와 친구분께서 서로의 성격을 잘 알고 계신다는 점이다. 따라서 어떤 행동을 하고 어떤 행동을 하지 말아야 하는지 알고 계신다. 이는 논쟁을 피하고 평소에 잘 지내는데 도움이 된다. 우정 덕분에 식당은 성공적으로 운영되고 있다.

Sample Response 2 Supporting Bernard

Although I understand the point Isabella makes, I agree with Bernard. Friends should never go into business together. It almost always ends in failure. My uncle and his friend started a store together. Times were tough, and they argued a lot. The business failed, and now they are no longer friends. That was very sad. Friends also may not have any business knowledge. So they might not actually be good at running a business. Instead of partnering with a friend, people should partner with someone who is good at business.

해석
Isabell의 논점은 이해하지만 나는 Bernard의 의견에 동의한다. 절대로 친구끼리 함께 사업을 해서는 안 된다. 그러면 거의 항상 실패로 끝나게 된다. 내 삼촌과 삼촌의 친구분은 함께 매장을 여셨다. 힘든 시기를 겪었으며 자주 논쟁을 벌이셨다. 사업은 실패했고 지금 두 분은 더 이상 친구 사이가 아니다. 매우 안타까운 일이었다. 또한 친구에게 사업에 대한 지식이 없을 수도 있다. 따라서 실제로 사업 운영에 능숙하지 못할 수도 있다. 친구와 동업을 하는 대신, 사람들은 사업에 능한 누군가와 동업을 해야 한다.

Unit 14 | Sociology II

Exercise 1 ·· p.114

Brainstorming & Outlining

A

Professor Trent

해석

요즘 사람들은 과거에 비해 더 많이 여행을 다닙니다. 일 년에 최소한 한 차례 여행을 하는 경우가 일반적이죠. 이러한 여행은 국내 여행일 수도 있고 해외 여행일 수도 있어요. 여러분은 여행을 할 때 국내 지역에 가는 것을 선호하나요, 아니면 해외 지역에 방문하는 것을 선호하나요? 그 이유는요?

B

Lionel

해석

저는 해외 여행을 해 본 적이 있지만 국내 여행을 더 선호해요. 우리나라는 아름다운 풍경으로 가득하기 때문에 방문할 만한 곳이 많아요. 저는 이곳에서 볼 수 있는 경이로운 자연 환경을 찾아가서 우리나라에 대해 알게 되는 것을 좋아합니다.

✐ Summary Notes: Lionel

1) beautiful scenery
2) Numerous
3) homeland
4) natural wonders

Sienna

해석

저는 우리나라에서 여행하는 것보다 다른 나라에 가는 것을 선호합니다. 방문할 만한 이국적인 곳들이 정말 많아요. 저는 역사적인 유적지를 방문하는 것도 좋아하고 유명한 랜드마크에 가 보는 것도 좋아해요. 유럽은 방문할 곳이 많아서 제가 가장 좋아하는 지역입니다.

✐ Summary Notes: Sienna

1) exotic lands
2) historical interest
3) landmarks
4) Europe
5) places

Organization
Supporting Lionel's Opinion

1 Sienna makes an appealing argument, but I prefer domestic trips like Lionel.
2 Lionel is correct about the many natural wonders in our country.
3 I love to visit these places, such as mountains and beaches.

4 I take photographs to make sure I never forget their beauty.
5 It is also important that domestic trips are cheaper than foreign ones.
6 My family can take more frequent trips by traveling in our own country.
7 We cannot afford to travel abroad frequently.
8 Those are the two reasons I prefer domestic travel.

Supporting Sienna's Opinion

1 I like the points both Lionel and Sienna make.
2 However, I agree with Sienna as I prefer to visit other countries.
3 My family visited England last year.
4 We saw landmarks like Buckingham Palace and famous places like Stonehenge.
5 It was an incredible trip.
6 Additionally, by traveling abroad, I can learn about foreign countries.
7 I like to see how people in other lands live.
8 I also enjoy trying to speak foreign languages.
9 I can only do these activities abroad.

Exercise 2 ·· p.117

Professor Cloniger

해석

이제 여러분이 대학 이후의 삶에 대해 생각해 보면 좋을 것 같군요. 학생들이 졸업을 하면 종종 일을 시작하게 됩니다. 이후에는 많은 사람들이 결혼을 해서 가정을 꾸리죠. 때로는 사람들은 일과 가족 중에서 선택을 해야만 합니다. 이 두 가지 중에서 어떤 것이 더 중요한가요? 그 이유는요?

Matthew

해석

두 가지 중에서는 일이 더 중요합니다. 저는 제 일에 대해 커다란 포부를 가지고 있으며, 언젠가 임원이 되기를 기대하고 있어요. 성공을 이루기 위해서는 오직 일에만 집중해야만 합니다. 여기에 다른 일이 방해가 되도록 놔둘 수는 없어요.

Stella

해석

다른 어떤 것보다 가족이 더 소중합니다. 저는 무엇보다 가족을 택할 거예요. 저는 언제든지 다른 일을 구할 수 있고, 다른 분야에서 경력을 쌓을 수도 있어요. 가족에게 나쁜 일이 일어나더라도 가족은 대체가 불가능합니다.

Sample Response 1 Supporting Matthew

I like how Stella thinks, but I would choose my career. Like Matthew, I too hope to excel in my chosen profession. I expect to become a CEO by the time I am thirty years old. I will need to dedicate all of my time and effort to work to achieve my goal. Additionally, when people have problems in their careers, it can affect them negatively. For instance, they can lose their homes and

become unhealthy. I do not want that to happen to me.
So I must dedicate my life to my career.

해석

Stella의 생각도 마음이 들지만 나는 일을 선택할 것이다. Matthew와 마찬가지로 나도 내가 선택한 직업에서 뛰어나고 싶다. 나는 30살 무렵에 대표 이사가 되기를 희망한다. 내 목적을 이루기 위해서는 모든 시간과 노력을 일에 바쳐야 할 것이다. 또한 사람들은 경력에서 문제를 겪는 경우 부정적인 영향을 받을 수 있다. 예를 들어 집을 잃을 수도 있고 건강이 악화될 수도 있다. 나는 그러한 일이 내게 일어나는 것을 원하지 않는다. 따라서 나는 일에 내 인생을 바쳐야 한다.

Sample Response 2 Supporting Stella

I could never put my career ahead of my family. Stella and I think the same way. I can always get a new career, but I have no desire to get a new family. As long as my family is doing well, I consider my life to be good. A job is just a way for me to make money. There are many ways to make money. So I do not concern myself about that. However, a happy family life means you have a good life. And that is all that matters.

해석

나는 절대로 가족보다 일을 우선시할 수 없을 것이다. Stella와 나는 같은 생각을 하고 있다. 나는 언제든지 새로운 일을 찾을 수 있지만, 새로운 가족을 얻고 싶지는 않다. 우리 가족이 잘 지내는 한 나는 내 삶이 좋은 삶이라고 생각한다. 나에게 일은 돈을 벌 수 있는 수단일 뿐이다. 돈을 벌 수 있는 방법은 많다. 따라서 나는 그에 대해 걱정하지 않는다. 하지만 행복한 가정 생활은 당신이 좋은 삶을 살고 있다는 의미를 나타낸다. 그리고 그것이 바로 중요한 점이다.

Unit 15 Education III

Exercise 1 .... p.120

Brainstorming & Outlining

A

Professor Eco

해석

고등학생들의 여름 방학은 최소 2개월인 경우가 많아요. 이때 많은 학생들이 돈을 벌고 경험을 쌓기 위해 아르바이트를 합니다. 개인 지도를 받은 것과 같이 다른 활동을 하는 학생들도 있고요. 여러분 생각으로 고등학생들은 어떤 활동을 해야 할까요? 그 이유는요?

B

Jessica

해석

여름은 고등학생들이 아르바이트를 하기에 이상적인 시기입니다. 다양한 일을 함으로써 남은 1년 동안 쓸 수 있는 돈을 벌 수 있어요. 또한 중요한 스킬을 가르

처 주는 경험을 쌓을 수도 있습니다. 이는 미래에 도움이 될 거예요.

🔖 **Summary Notes: Jessica**

1) spending money
2) remainder
3) various jobs
4) experience
5) important skills
6) future

Rudy

해석

고등학생들은 그러한 기회를 이용해서 다른 활동을 해야 합니다. 개인 교습을 받음으로써 악기 연주를 배울 수도 있을 거예요. 또한 미술 교습을 받거나 외국어를 배울 수도 있고요. 수업이 없기 때문에 새로운 기술이나 능력을 배우는 일에 집중할 수 있습니다.

🔖 **Summary Notes: Rudy**

1) musical instrument
2) private lessons
3) art lessons
4) foreign language
5) new skill or ability

Organization
Supporting Jessica's Opinion

1 I like both options, but working part time is the better choice.
2 High school students should earn spending money.
3 Then, they will not have to ask their parents for money.
4 This will prepare them for their adult lives.
5 Another reason is that students can learn life skills from their jobs.
6 They can learn to be on time, to keep a schedule, and to work for others.
7 They can also learn skills specific to their jobs.
8 They will be useful when students start their careers.
9 That is why students should work part time.

Supporting Rudy's Opinion

1 I agree with Rudy and think high school students should do activities other than working.
2 Learning an instrument or a new language, as Rudy suggests, would be great.
3 My brother learned the piano last summer, and my sister studied Chinese.
4 Those skills have helped them both.
5 In addition, unlike working, learning new skills does not take many hours.
6 Students should enjoy their summer vacation by having fun.

7 They should not <u>work several hours each day</u>.

8 They can <u>do that after they graduate</u>.

9 Instead, they ought to <u>spend a bit of time learning a new skill</u>.

Exercise 2 ··· p.123

Professor Peters

해석

다음 주 월요일에는 자원봉사에 대해 논의할 거예요. 생각해 보아야 할 토론 게시판의 주제를 알려 드리죠. 많은 학교들이 학생들로 하여금 자유 시간에 급식소, 노숙자 쉼터, 혹은 기타 장소에서 자원봉사를 할 것을 요구하고 있어요. 학생들이 자원봉사를 해야 한다고 생각하나요? 그 이유는요?

Phillip

해석

학교는 반드시 학생들에게 자원봉사를 시켜야 해요. 학생들은 사회 내 얼마나 많은 사람이 불행하게 사는지 보아야 합니다. 따라서 가난하고, 실직 상태이고, 집이 없는 사람들이 다니는 곳에서 자원봉사를 해야 합니다. 그러한 곳에서 자원봉사를 하면 학생들이 인생에 관한 교훈을 많이 배울 수 있을 거예요.

Fiona

해석

학교가 학생들에게 자원봉사 활동을 강제하는 것은 잘못된 일입니다. 어찌되었든 자원봉사라는 말에 사람들이 원해서 어떤 일을 한다는 의미가 담겨 있으니까요. 학생들이 강제로 자원봉사를 한다면 대부분이 소극적일 것이며 근무 태도도 좋지 못할 거예요. 그들에게 어떤 식으로든 도움이 되지 않을 것입니다.

Sample Response 1 Supporting Phillip

I agree with Phillip and think schools should make students volunteer. As he mentions, students can benefit from helping the unfortunate. They can learn compassion and how to take care of others. Students can also volunteer in ways that can benefit their future careers. For instance, students thinking of becoming doctors can volunteer at hospitals. Those considering becoming teachers can volunteer as tutors. Their volunteer work will provide them with valuable job experience. There are clearly many benefits to students doing volunteer work.

해석

나는 Phillip의 의견에 동의하며 학교가 학생들에게 자원봉사를 시켜야 한다고 생각한다. 그가 언급한 것처럼 학생들은 불행한 사람들을 도움으로써 혜택을 받을 수 있다. 동정심을 기르고 다른 사람을 어떻게 돌보아야 하는지 배울 수 있다. 학생들은 또한 미래의 자신의 경력에 도움이 되는 식으로 자원봉사를 할 수도 있다. 예를 들어 의사가 되려는 학생들은 병원에서 자원봉사를 할 수 있다. 교사를 고려 중인 학생들은 개인 교사로서 자원봉사를 할 수 있다. 이들은 자원봉사로 업무와 관련된 귀중한 경험을 하게 될 것이다. 자원봉사를 하는 학생들에게는 분명 많은 혜택이 돌아간다.

Sample Response 2 Supporting Fiona

Fiona is correct in arguing that schools should not force students to volunteer. Volunteer work should be voluntary. This means that students should want to do it, not be forced to do it. People forced to do activities will be angry and bitter and will not benefit. Schools should also remember that students have various interests after school. Some take private lessons while others may play sports or study music or art. These individuals may not have time to volunteer. It would therefore be wrong to make students do volunteer work.

해석

학교가 학생들에게 자원봉사를 강요해서는 안 된다는 Fiona의 주장이 옳다. 자원봉사 업무는 자발적인 것이어야 한다. 이는 학생들이 자원봉사를, 강제에 의해서가 아니라, 하고 싶어해야 한다는 점을 의미한다. 강제로 활동을 하는 사람들은 기분이 상하고 억울해 할 것이며 혜택을 받지 못할 것이다. 또한 학교는 학생들이 방과 후 다양한 활동을 한다는 점을 기억해야 한다. 개인 교습을 받는 학생도 있고 스포츠를 하거나 음악 및 미술 공부를 하는 학생들도 있을 것이다. 이러한 개인들에게는 자원봉사를 할 시간이 없다. 따라서 학생들에게 자원봉사를 시키는 것은 부당한 일이다.

Unit 16 Sociology III

Exercise 1 ··· p.126

Brainstorming & Outlining

A

Professor Windsor

해석

다음 주에는 우리나라의 인구 문제에 대해 논의할 예정이에요. 이에 관한 여러분들의 생각을 알고 싶군요. 많은 대도시의 중심가에 인구가 밀집되어 있습니다. 이로써 교통 체증 및 높은 집세와 같은 문제들이 발생하고 있죠. 인구 문제를 경감시키기 위해 도시들이 어떻게 할 수 있을까요? 그렇게 생각하는 이유는 무엇인가요?

B

Ashley

해석

도시들은 사람들에게 교외 지역에 사는 것을 장려해야 합니다. 그렇게 하면 사람들이 직장이 위치한 도시 근처에서 살게 될 거예요. 실제로 그러한 도시 안에서 사는 것이 아니고요. 지하철 및 버스와 같은 대중 교통을 개선시킴으로써 도시는 교외 지역을 보다 매력적인 곳으로 만들 수 있습니다. 그러면 도시의 인구가 감소할 거예요.

✏️ **Summary Notes: Ashley**

1) <u>live in suburbs</u>

2) <u>work</u>

3) <u>live</u>

4) <u>public transportation</u>

5) more appealing

6) decline

Brian

해석

몇몇 도시에는 비어 있는 부지가 많습니다. 예를 들어 여러 동네에 버려진 건물이나 주택들이 존재해요. 도시들은 이 부지로 무언가를 해야 합니다. 더 많은 주거 시설을 지을 수도 있을 거예요. 아니면 이러한 장소를 공원으로 만들 수도 있을 것이고요. 그렇게 하면 도시가 보다 쾌적하게 될 것이며, 인구 밀도도 낮아 보일 거예요.

✏ Summary Notes: Brian

1) empty land
2) buildings and houses
3) land
4) Construct
5) parks
6) comfortable
7) populated

Organization

Supporting New Ideas: Making Buildings Taller

1   I really like the suggestions by Ashley and Brian.
2   I would like to propose something different though.
3   Cities should construct more apartment buildings, and they should make the buildings taller.
4   My city has plenty of apartments, but most are only twenty floors high.
5   They need to be thirty or forty floors high instead.
6   The reason is that these buildings will hold more people while using a small amount of land.
7   This will open up more space in cities.
8   Cities can reclaim this extra land for roads or parks.
9   Then, cities will not be so overpopulated.

Supporting New Ideas: Letting People Work at Home

1   While Ashley and Brian have some clever ideas, I have a different one.
2   Cities should encourage employers to let people work from home.
3   This will immediately reduce traffic, which is a major problem in overpopulated cities.
4   Fewer people will ride on buses and subways, too.
5   So they will not be so crowded.
6   Another benefit will be that some people who work from home will move out of cities.
7   They will live in suburbs or other places.
8   As a result, the populations of cities will decrease.
9   This will make urban life better for the remaining people.

Professor Caldwell

해석

다음 수업에서는 사람들을 어떻게 더 행복하게 만들 수 있는지에 대해 이야기할 것입니다. 오늘날 많은 사람들이 불행해 합니다. 직업, 가정사, 그리고 기타 문제들 때문에 그렇게 생각하는 것이죠. 행복을 증진시키기 위해 사람들이 어떻게 해야 한다고 생각하나요? 왜 그렇게 생각하나요?

Tucker

해석

사람들은 더 많은 시간을 써서 자기 자신에게 집중해야 해요. 예를 들어 너무나 많은 사람들이 주로 일에 대해서 생각을 합니다. 일찍 일어나서, 하루 종일 일하고, 밤늦게 집에 돌아오죠. 이는 행복의 공식이 아닙니다. 일에 대해 덜 생각하고 자기 자신에 대해 더 생각을 하면 사람들이 보다 행복해질 거예요.

Sheila

해석

저는 사람들이 더 많은 취미를 가져야 한다고 생각합니다. 집에 머물면서 TV를 보거나 컴퓨터 게임을 하는 대신에 다른 활동을 해야 해요. 하이킹을 할 수도 있고, 책을 읽을 수 있고, 아니면 그림을 배울 수도 있을 거예요. 그와 비슷한 활동을 하면 행복 지수가 올라갈 것입니다.

Sample Response 1 Supporting New Ideas: Becoming Closer to One's Family

Both Tucker and Sheila argue that people should do more activities for themselves. I believe they are correct. In my case, I think people should become closer to their families. So many families do not talk or even eat meals together nowadays. I think that must be depressing. Instead, people need to take time to be with the people they live with. They should eat meals with their families. They should talk to their families, and they should do various free-time activities with their families. In those ways, people could improve their happiness.

해석

Tucker와 Sheila 모두 사람들이 스스로를 위한 활동을 더 많이 해야 한다고 주장한다. 나는 그들이 옳다고 믿는다. 내 경우, 나는 사람들이 자신의 가족과 더 친밀하게 지내야 한다고 생각한다. 오늘날 너무 많은 가족들이 이야기를 나누지 않거나 심지어 같이 식사도 하지 않는다. 틀림없이 우울한 일이라고 생각된다. 대신 사람들은 시간을 내서 같이 살고 있는 사람들과 함께 있어야 한다. 가족과 함께 식사를 해야 한다. 가족들과 이야기를 나누고, 가족들과 함께 다양한 여가 활동을 해야 한다. 그렇게 함으로써 사람들은 행복을 증진시킬 수 있을 것이다.

Sample Response 2 Supporting New Ideas: Taking More Vacations

I like the comments that Tucker and Sheila make. To build on their arguments, I would say that people need to take more vacations. My parents have not taken a vacation in many years. They are both always busy working at their jobs. They are also very unhappy. They could make themselves happy by taking a trip. In addition, when people travel, they enjoy a slower pace of life. Most people's lives today are too hectic due to work or school. If people travel, they can relax and slow down. That will instantly make them much happier.

해석

나는 Tucker와 Sheila의 주장이 마음에 든다. 그들의 주장에 추가해서 나는 사람들이 휴가를 더 많이 가야한다고 말하고 싶다. 우리 부모님께서는 여러 해 동안 휴가를 가지 않으셨다. 두 분 모두 항상 직장에서 일하느라 바쁘시다. 또한 매우 불행해 하신다. 부모님들은 여행을 함으로써 스스로를 행복하게 만드실 수 있을 것이다. 게다가 여행을 하면 보다 느린 속도의 삶을 즐길 수 있다. 오늘날 대부분의 사람들의 삶은 일 혹은 학업으로 인해 지나치게 빡빡하다. 여행을 하면 휴식을 취하면서 여유를 누릴 수 있다. 그러면 그 즉시 훨씬 더 많은 행복감을 느끼게 될 것이다.

Actual Test

Actual Test 01   p.134

Task 1

Reading

해석

프레리도그는 토끼 크기의 설치류로 청솔모 및 다람쥐와 친척 관계이다. 이 동물의 원산지는 북아메리카의 평원이다. 최근 몇 십년 동안, 주로 인간의 활동 때문에, 이들의 수는 최대 95%까지 급격히 줄어들었다. 하지만 이들은 가치가 거의 없고 실제로 해를 끼칠 수도 있기 때문에 이들을 보호할 필요는 없다.

먼저 프레리도그는 소를 키우는 목장 지역에서 산다. 이러한 많은 곳에서는 비가 오는 경우가 드물다. 그 결과 때때로 풀이 잘 자라지 않는다. 프레리도그는 막대한 양의 풀을 뜯어먹는다. 따라서 프레리도그와 같은 곳에서 사는 소들이 풀을 뜯어먹을 때 충분한 양의 먹이를 섭취하지 못할 수 있다. 이는 소들에게 피해를 주며 목장 주인들이 금전적인 손실을 보도록 만든다.

두 번째 요점은 프레리도그가 먹이 사슬에 있어서 그다지 중요하지 않다는 점이다. 이들을 먹이로 삼는 동물들, 예컨대 늑대와 코요테들이 있다. 하지만 프레리도그는 비교적 크기가 작다. 이는 크기가 큰 포식자들이 프레리도그만 사냥해서는 살아갈 수가 없다는 점을 의미한다. 이러한 이유들 때문에 정부가 프레리도그의 개체수를 증가시키기 위해 노력을 기울여야 할 필요는 없다.

Listening

Script 🎧 02-03

M Professor: This . . . is a picture of a prairie dog. This lovable creature is not an endangered species yet. However, humans are causing its numbers to decline rapidly. That's bad news because we really need to preserve this animal since it is an important species in its ecosystems.

Now, uh, some people claim that prairie dogs compete with cattle for grass. Let me tell you something . . . That's nonsense. Cattle do not graze on the plains. They are raised on farms, where they have plenty of food. In actuality, uh, grass grows very well in places where prairie dogs have their burrows. Their burrows also take in water during heavy rains, so they help prevent soil erosion.

In addition, prairie dogs are vital members of their ecosystems. First, they dig extensive burrows, but they aren't the only animals that live in them. Prairie dogs reside in their burrows alongside some species of snakes and even owls and rabbits. Hawks, ferrets, coyotes, and other animals hunt them, too. So they are valuable sources of food for many animals that live in the plains. Without prairie dogs, the land and the animals in the plains would look very different.

M Professor: 여기에… 프레리도그의 사진이 있어요. 이 사랑스러운 생물은 아직 멸종 위기종이 아닙니다. 하지만 인간이 그 숫자를 급격히 감소시키고 있죠. 이는 나쁜 소식인데, 그 이유는 이 동물이 생태계에서 중요한 종이라서 이를 꼭 보호해야 하기 때문입니다.

자, 어, 어떤 사람들은 프레리도그가 풀을 두고 소들과 경쟁을 한다고 주장해요. 제가 말씀을 드리면… 말도 안 됩니다. 소들은 평원에서 풀을 뜯어먹지 않아요. 먹이가 풍부한 농장에서 길러지죠. 실제로, 어, 프레리도그가 굴을 파는 지역에서는 풀들이 매우 잘 자랍니다. 또한 폭우가 내리는 동안에는 물이 굴로 들어가기 때문에 굴은 토양 침식을 예방하는데 도움을 주어요.

또한 프레리도그는 생태계의 매우 중요한 구성원입니다. 먼저 이들은 넓게 뻗친 굴을 파는데, 여기에는 이 동물만 사는 것이 아니에요. 굴에서 프레리도그도 살지만 몇몇 종의 뱀과 심지어 올빼미와 토끼도 삽니다. 또한 매, 흰담비, 코요테, 그리고 기타 동물들이 이들을 사냥해요. 그래서 이들은 평원에 사는 많은 동물들에게 귀중한 먹이원이 됩니다. 프레리도그가 없다면 평원의 토지와 동물들의 상황이 크게 달라질 거예요.

The lecture and the reading passage are both about prairie dogs. While the author of the reading passage argues that prairie dogs do not need to be saved, the professor feels differently.

The professor first remarks that prairie dogs do not compete with cattle for grass. This contradicts the point made in the reading passage. The writer claims that prairie dogs eat so much grass that cattle cannot find enough food to eat, which makes ranchers lose money. The professor, however, says that cattle eat on farms and that grass grows well where prairie dogs live.

Next, the professor casts doubt on the statement in the reading passage that prairie dogs are not important in the food chain. He points out that many animals, including hawks, coyotes, and ferrets, prey on prairie dogs. He also notes that numerous animals live together with prairie dogs in their burrows.

The professor therefore shows that prairie dogs are important parts of their ecosystems.

강의와 읽기 지문 모두 프레리도그에 관한 것이다. 읽기 지문의 저자는 프레리도그를 보호할 필요가 없다고 주장하지만 교수의 생각은 다르다.

교수는 먼저 프레리도그가 풀을 두고 소들과 경쟁하지 않는다고 언급한다. 이는 읽기 지문에서 제기된 논점과 반대되는 것이다. 글쓴이는 프레리도그가 풀을 너무 많이 먹어서 소들이 충분한 양의 먹이를 찾지 못하게 되고 이로써 농장 주인들이 금전적인 손실을 입는다고 주장한다. 하지만 교수는 소들이 농장에서 먹이를 먹으며 프레리도그가 사는 곳의 풀들은 잘 자란다고 말한다.

다음으로 교수는 프레리도그가 먹이 사슬에서 중요하지 않다는 읽기 지문의 주장에 의문을 제기한다. 그는 매, 코요테, 그리고 흰담비를 포함하여 많은 동물들이 프레리도그를 먹이로 삼는다고 지적한다. 또한 다수의 동물들이 프레리도그와 함께 이들의 굴 속에서 산다고 언급한다.

따라서 교수는 프레리도그가 생태계의 중요한 일부라는 점을 보여 준다.

Task 2

Professor Hammond

요즘 지구의 환경이 사람들의 주요 관심사입니다. 토양 오염, 대기 오염, 그리고 수질 오염을 포함하여 온갖 종류의 오염이 지구를 더럽히고 있어요. 그 결과 모든 곳에서 많은 문제들이 일어나고 있습니다. 환경을 깨끗하게 하기 위한 최선의 방법은 무엇일까요? 그 이유는요?

Lisa

사람들이 자기 주변을 깨끗이 해야 합니다. 너무나 많은 사람들이 땅에 쓰레기를 버리는 모습을 보이고 있어요. 그렇게 하면 안 됩니다. 쓰레기통을 이용해야 하죠. 어딘가에서 쓰레기를 본다면 쓰레기를 주워서 버리면 됩니다. 작은 행동들이 모여서 커다란 결과를 이루어낼 수 있어요.

Thomas

사람들은 오염 유발자에게 항의를 해야 해요. 많은 오염 유발자들은 대규모 공장입니다. 대기에 해로운 연기를 내보내고 물속에 화학 물질들을 버리죠. 항의를 함으로써 이러한 오염 유발자들이 자신의 방식을 바꾸도록 강요할 수 있습니다. 그 결과로 환경이 보다 깨끗해질 거예요.

Supporting New Ideas: Recycling More

Both Lisa and Thomas have great ideas, but I support doing something else. I believe that people ought to recycle more. Landfills around the world are becoming full. The main reason is that people do not recycle. By recycling, landfills will fill up more slowly. In addition, by recycling, we can reuse many natural resources. Then, we can mine less for minerals and cut down fewer trees. This will help the environment a tremendous amount. As a result, the Earth will be much cleaner and better to live on.

Lisa와 Thomas 모두 훌륭한 아이디어를 가지고 있지만 나는 다른 일을 하는 것을 지지한다. 나는 사람들이 재활용을 더 많이 해야 한다고 생각한다. 전 세계의 매립지가 포화 상태에 이르고 있다. 주된 이유는 사람들이 재활용을 하지 않기 때문이다. 재활용을 하면 매립지가 보다 천천히 포화 상태에 이를 것이다. 또한 재활용을 함으로써 많은 천연 자원들을 재사용할 수 있다. 그러면 광물을 덜 캐낼 수 있고, 나무도 덜 베어낼 수 있다. 이는 환경에 막대한 도움이 될 것이다. 그 결과 지구는 훨씬 더 깨끗하고 살기 좋은 곳이 될 것이다.

Supporting New Ideas: Reducing Fossil Fuel Use

While Lisa and Thomas have proposed interesting solutions, I prefer another action. A lot of pollution is caused by the burning of coal, gas, and oil. People should demand that we use these energy sources less. That would immediately reduce the amount of air, water, and ground pollution. People also need to insist that we use clean sources of energy. For instance, hydroelectric energy from water is clean, and so is nuclear power. By telling our governments to use clean energy sources, we can make the environment of the entire planet cleaner.

해석

Lisa와 Thomas가 흥미로운 해결책을 제시했지만 나는 다른 행동을 선호한다. 많은 오염이 석탄, 가스, 그리고 석유를 연소시켜서 발생한다. 사람들은 이러한 에너지원을 덜 사용하자고 주장해야 한다. 그러면 즉시 대기 오염, 수질 오염, 그리고 토양 오염의 양이 줄어들 것이다. 사람들은 또한 청정 에너지원을 사용하자고 주장해야 한다. 예를 들어 물에서 나오는 수력 에너지는 깨끗하며 원자력도 마찬가지이다. 정부에 청정 에너지원을 사용하라고 말함으로써 지구 전체의 환경을 보다 깨끗하게 만들 수 있다.

Actual Test 02
p.142

Task 1

Reading

해석

전 세계 바다에서 거대한 호화 유람선을 목격할 수 있다. 많은 유람선들이 미국과 캐나다의 서쪽 해안으로 올라온다. 그런 다음 알래스카의 보다 북쪽 지역까지 항해를 계속한다. 승객들은 이러한 여행을 즐기지만 유람선과 그 승객들은 환경과 지역 주민들에게 피해를 끼치고 있다.

유람선이 움직이기 위해서는 엄청난 양의 연료가 필요하다. 엔진에서 연소되는 석유에서는 대기와 수질을 오염시키는 해로운 입자들이 배출된다. 이는 또한 수많은 해양 생물 및 조류들을 죽거나 아프게 만든다. 또 다른 문제는 연료가 연소됨으로써 눈과 얼음이 녹는다는 점이다. 이 또한 북극의 환경에 부정적인 영향을 미칠 수 있다.

항해를 하는 동안 유람선은 캐나다와 알래스카의 항구에 빈번하게 정박을 한다. 이러한 정박지 중 일부는 작은 마을이다. 일부 경우에는 마을에 사는 사람보다 유람선에 탄 승객들이 더 많을 때도 있다. 배에서 내린 승객들은 종종 지역 주민들에게 민폐를 끼친다. 막대한 양의 물품들을 소비하고 다량의 쓰레기를 만들어 낸다. 그들의 방문은 지역 주민들에게 도움이 되는 것이 아니라 오히려 상당한 피해를 주고 있다.

Listening

Script 🎧 02-06

W Professor: Last summer, I went on a cruise up the western coast of Canada and the United States. I know many people dislike these tours and claim they're destructive to the environment and people. But the cruise I went on was nothing of the sort.

For instance, my cruise ship used a special kind of fuel for its engines. The oil had a low sulfur content, which made its emissions less harmful to the environment. Yes, it created some pollution, but the amount was much less than what's made by most cruise ships. In addition, on the cruise, we saw melting glaciers and learned about the struggles of various animals, such as polar bears, to survive. This provided passengers with a valuable education on the environment.

Heading north, we stopped at a couple of small towns. Every passenger was not permitted to disembark simultaneously. That would have been too, uh, too overwhelming for the townspeople. Instead, some passengers disembarked. When they returned, others were allowed to go onshore. This method took the needs and desires of the townspeople into consideration. They were quite happy, especially considering the large amounts of money many passengers spent in those towns.

해석

W Professor: 지난 여름에 저는 유람선 여행으로 캐나다와 미국의 서쪽 해안에 갔습니다. 많은 사람들이 그러한 투어를 좋아하지 않으며 그러한 투어가 환경과 사람들에게 해를 끼친다고 주장한다는 점은 저도 알고 있어요. 하지만 제가 했던 유람선 여행은 전혀 그렇지가 않았습니다.

예를 들어 제가 탔던 유람선의 엔진에는 특별한 연료가 사용되었어요. 유황이 적게 들어 있는 석유였는데, 이로 인해 덜 해로운 물질이 방출되었죠. 네, 어느 정도 오염은 발생시켰지만 그 양은 대부분의 유람선에서 만들어지는 것보다 훨씬 적은 양이었습니다. 또한 유람에서 저희는 녹고 있는 빙하도 보았고 다양한 동물들이, 예컨대 북극곰이 생존하기 위해 고분분투한다는 점도 알게 되었어요. 이로써 승객들은 환경에 관한 소중한 교육을 받을 수 있었죠.

저희는 북쪽으로 향하는 동안 두어 곳의 작은 마을에서 정박을 했습니다. 그 즉시 모든 승객들의 하선이 허용된 것은 아니었어요. 그랬다면 마을 사람들이 감당하기에 너무나, 어, 너무나 힘들었을 것입니다. 대신 일부 승객들만 하선을 했어요. 그들이 돌아오자 다른 사람들이 상륙을 할 수 있었습니다. 이러한 방법은 마을 사람들의 요구와 바람을 고려한 것이었어요. 그들은, 특히 많은 승객들이 그들의 마을에서 쓰고 간 돈이 엄청났다는 점을 고려할 때, 상당히 만족해 했습니다.

Sample Response

The reading passage and the lecture discuss visits by cruise ships to the western coast of Alaska and the United States. The reading passage argues that these cruises are harmful, but the professor challenges those claims.

The professor states that her cruise ship used fuel with a low sulfur content. This reduced the amount of pollution created. This goes against the point in the reading that argues that cruise ships create too much pollution by burning fuel for their engines. The professor adds that passengers on her cruise learned about glaciers and animals such as polar bears. In that way, they were educated about environmental issues.

For her second point, the professor discusses stops at small towns during the cruise. Although the reading passage notes that townspeople get overwhelmed by these visits, the professor disagrees. She mentions that passengers from her ship went onshore in groups. This avoided causing problems for the townspeople. The passengers also spent plenty of money, which helped the townspeople financially.

The professor therefore disputes the claims made in the reading passage.

읽기 지문과 강의 모두 유람선으로 알래스카 및 미국의 서쪽 해안가를 여행하는 것에 대해 논의하고 있다. 읽기 지문은 이러한 유람선 여행이 해를 끼친다고 주장하지만 교수는 그러한 주장을 반박한다.

교수는 자신이 탔던 유람선이 유황이 적게 들어 있는 연료를 사용했다고 말한다. 이로써 발생하는 오염 물질의 양이 줄어들었다. 이는 유람선 엔진에 사용되는 연료가 연소되면 너무 많은 오염 물질이 발생한다는 읽기 지문의 주장과 상반되는 것이다. 교수는 덧붙여서 유람선의 승객들이 빙하와 북극곰 같은 동물들에 대해 배울 수 있었다고 말한다. 그런 식으로 승객들은 환경 문제에 관한 교육을 받았다.

두 번째로 교수는 유람선 여행 도중에 작은 마을에서 정박한 일에 대해 논의한다. 읽기 지문은 마을 사람들이 이러한 방문을 감당하지 못한다고 말하지만 교수는 이에 동의하지 않는다. 그녀는 배의 승객들이 그룹별로 상륙을 했다고 언급한다. 이로써 마을 사람들에게 문제를 일으키지 않을 수 있었다. 승객들은 또한 많은 돈을 썼는데, 이는 마을 사람들에게 금전적으로 도움이 되었다.

따라서 교수는 읽기 지문에서 제기된 주장을 반박하고 있다.

Task 2

Professor Drago

소비자 행동에 관한 논의를 계속하고자 합니다. 요즘 인터넷 덕분에 사람들이 집에서 쇼핑하는 일이 가능해졌습니다. 따라서 온라인 쇼핑이 보다 일반적이 되었죠. 여러분은 온라인으로 물품을 구매하는 것을 선호하나요? 아니면 매장에 가서 쇼핑을 하는 것을 선호하나요? 그 이유는요?

Leslie

저는 온라인 쇼핑을 크게 선호하는 편입니다. 일주일에 최소한 한 번은 온라인으로 쇼핑을 해요. 집에서 쇼핑을 할 수 있다는 편리함이 정말 좋습니다. 또한 저는 붐비는 사람들과 판매를 강요하는 직원들을 마주하는 것이 싫어요. 온라인으로 쇼핑을 하는 경우에는 그런 문제가 없습니다.

Ferdinand

저도 전에 온라인 쇼핑을 해 본 적이 있지만 저는 이를 그다지 좋아하지 않습니다. 오히려 매장을 방문해서 쇼핑하는 것이 좋아요. 저는 의류를 구입할 때 제품을 만지고 입어보는 편입니다. 슈퍼마켓에서 선택할 수 있는 것들을 보고 결정을 내리죠.

Sample Response 1 Supporting Leslie

I agree with Leslie that online shopping is the better way. I too do not like dealing with salespeople. They follow shoppers around and try to convince them to make purchases. When I shop online, nobody pressures me to buy something. Another benefit of online shopping is that there are many sales and discount opportunities. I often get notifications from stores about sales. I can then check their websites and make purchases easily. Many stores do not charge for shipping, so that makes the prices even lower. These are two of the benefits of online shopping.

나는 온라인 쇼핑이 더 나은 방식이라는 Leslie의 의견에 동의한다. 나 역시 판매 직원들을 상대하는 것을 좋아하지 않는다. 그들은 쇼핑객들을 쫓아다니면서 물건을 사도록 설득하려고 한다. 온라인에서 쇼핑을 하면 누구도 내게 무엇을 사라고 압박하지 않는다. 온라인 쇼핑의 또 다른 이점은 세일과 할인 혜택이 많다는 것이다. 나는 종종 매장으로부터 세일에 관한 알림을 받는다. 그러면 웹사이트를 확인해서 쉽게 구매를 할 수가 있다. 많은 매장들이 배송비를 부과하지 않는데, 이로써 가격이 훨씬 더 낮아지게 된다. 이러한 점들은 온라인 쇼핑의 두 가지 이점이다.

Sample Response 2 Supporting Ferdinand

While Leslie makes some good points, I side with Ferdinand. I prefer shopping at stores to shopping online. Ferdinand mentions shopping for clothes. The best way to do that is to shop at a store to try clothes on. I often buy clothes, and I need to make sure they fit. Shopping at a store is the way to do that. I also sometimes require help from salespeople. I ask questions about items, and they provide answers. For instance, they can show me how to use various appliances. You can only get service like that by shopping at a store.

Leslie가 좋은 지적을 했지만 나는 Ferdinand와 같은 입장이다. 나는 온라인으로 쇼핑을 하는 것보다 매장에서 쇼핑하는 것을 선호한다. Ferdinand는 의류 쇼핑에 대해 언급한다. 의류를 쇼핑하는 가장 좋은 방법은 매장에서 쇼핑을 해서 옷을 입어보는 것이다. 나는 종종 의류를 구입하는데, 옷이 맞는지를 확인해야 한다. 매장에서 쇼핑을 하는 것이 그럴 수 있는 방법이다. 또한 때때로 판매 직원들의 도움이 필요한 경우가 있다. 내가 제품에 대한 질문을 하면 그들이 답을 해준다. 예를 들어 그들이 다양한 전자 기기들의 사용법을 알려 줄 수도 있다. 그러한 서비스는 매장에서 쇼핑을 하는 경우에만 받을 수 있는 것이다.

MEMO

MEMO